Abundance
for
Beginners

About the Author

Ellen Peterson is a psychotherapist and intuitive healer who has provided counseling services to individuals, couples, families, and groups for fifteen years. She owns AVENUES Counseling Center in Ithaca, New York.

Peterson is also the author of *Choosing Joy, Creating Abundance: Practical Tools for Manifesting Your Desires.* She enjoys teaching others how to fully step into abundant living, and she facilitates an abundance workshop entitled *EnRiching Your Life.* She also leads retreats focusing on personal growth. For further information about Peterson and her workshops, please visit http://www.ellenpeterson.com.

Peterson has been interviewed on television and radio, and is a member of the National Association of Social Workers and the Heart-Centered Therapies Association.

Abundance
for
Beginners

Simple Strategies for
Successful Living

Ellen
Peterson

Llewellyn Publications
Woodbury, Minnesota

First Edition
First Printing, 2007
Book design by Steffani Chambers
Cover design by Gavin Dayton Duffy
Editing by Brett Fechheimer
Cover photo © 2007 by Veer

Llewellyn is a registered trademark of Llewellyn Worldwide, Ltd.

Library of Congress Cataloging-in-Publication Data
    Peterson, Ellen, 1964-
      Abundance for beginners : simple strategies for successful living / Ellen Peterson. — 1st ed.
        p. cm.
      Includes bibliographical references.
      ISBN-13: 978-0-7387-0770-9
      ISBN-10: 0-7387-0770-8
        1. Self-actualization (Psychology) 2. Success—Psychological aspects. I. Title
      BF637.S4P448 2007
      158.1—dc22   2006048772

Llewellyn Publications
A Division of Llewellyn Worldwide, Ltd.
2143 Wooddale Drive, Dept. 0-7387-0770-8
Woodbury, MN 55125-2989, U.S.A.
www.llewellyn.com
Printed in the United States of America

Also by Ellen Peterson
Choosing Joy, Creating Abundance:
Practical Tools for Manifesting Your Desires
(Llewellyn Publications, 2004)

CONTENTS

ACKNOWLEDGMENTS

I must first thank God for granting me another dream come true. He continues to be the best co-author that anyone could ever have.

I give thanks to my loving family: Jamie, Kelci, and Marissa, who provide me with the love and support that is necessary in making a dream a reality. I thank my parents, Charles and Doris Peterson, for the gift of life that provides me with unlimited opportunities to learn and to teach.

I am blessed with the extensions of love from my siblings, Maureen Hanak, Barry Peterson, and Karan Cooney, and their children, to whom I have lovingly dedicated this book: Steven, Joshua, and Timothy Hanak; Kristen Garcia; Kerri D'Amico; Steven, Lisa, Jeff, and Jackie Peterson; and Brianna and Richard Cooney. May this book serve to guide you onto the path of abundance and allow you to experience rich and rewarding lives.

I wish to thank my many clients, particularly those who have traveled the Personal Transformation Intensive™ path with me. Together we have moved through the obstacles that would otherwise prevent us from embracing the endless possibilities in life. Thank you to the dedicated staff at Llewellyn Worldwide, who have provided me with opportunities to write and to create in ways that were once unimaginable to me. In addition, I wish to thank Karen Howarth for her creative expertise in both writing and enjoying life. Thank you for making the editing process pleasurable.

May your personal and professional lives be peaceful, happy, and overflowing with abundance. May your path open to new opportunities, creating a life in which all your dreams come true!

INTRODUCTION

What I believe is that, by proper effort, we make the future almost anything we want to make it.

Charles F. Ketterling

You are at the crossroads of your life. Your life has brought you to a new starting point and it is here that you must now choose your direction.

We often say to any person approaching a new beginning: "This is the time of your life." That may be a true statement, but there are many wonderful times in your life that will prove noteworthy. Graduations, weddings, the purchase of a new home, the arrival of a new baby, a job promotion, a move to a new area, and the start of a business all represent wonderful times in each of our lives.

New beginnings are exciting but also scary; they are times of creation. They are times to dream, to envision your ideal life. The choices that you make at these crossroads will greatly affect your life. Will you choose a life of ease or a life of struggle? When you are at a crossroads in your life, you are embarking on something new, something incredible. You are filled with excitement and apprehension. Which way do you go?

Some people hold on to dreams that originated in childhood. They hold a picture in their mind of their perfect wedding or their ideal career. They speculate about the number of children they will have in the family they will create. For visual people, dreaming is the easy part; they can easily visualize their dreams and desires, down to the finest detail. On the other hand, there are many people who have difficulty with visualization and who struggle in the process of developing their dreams.

Is it important to be able to visualize your dreams? The answer depends on you. The truth is that you have desires. There are no doubt numerous things you would like to attract in your life—such as money, meaningful work, loving long-term relationships, a nicer home or vehicle, life satisfaction, joy, and fulfillment. To begin the process of attracting abundance into your life, you must simply want to attract an abundant life. It is as simple as *wanting* abundance.

Abundance for Beginners marks the beginning of a wonderful, fruitful journey toward your joyful and abundant life. This book will walk you through simple steps toward manifesting your dreams and desires, and toward creating a life of abundance.

Dreams begin as mere ideas. Are you able to hold an idea in your mind? Do you have an idea of what you would like to have and experience in your life?

Without a doubt, something wonderful is about to happen.

PART ONE

Abundance Is Possible

CHAPTER ONE

Beyond Beginner's Luck

Destiny is not a matter of chance;
it is a matter of choice.

William Jennings Bryan

You are a beginner to abundance. If you are like many beginners, you feel awkward or uncomfortable with this simple fact. You would prefer to already know how to do something, as opposed to having to learn.

Beginners are anxious and unsure of how to proceed, and would rather skip ahead to already knowing so they can avoid the negative feelings associated with beginner status. Some people might even skip this first chapter in their mission to find immediate answers. They don't want to *learn* how to do something. They just want to be able to do it.

This urge is exemplified by the people who don't like to read directions. Such people just want to put an item together; they don't want to read about *how* to do so. In an effort to avoid the awkwardness of not knowing, they jump ahead and risk what they fear the most: failure. When they make a mistake, they spend time redoing what they've done incorrectly and get angry at themselves for not knowing how to put the item together.

That approach is a recipe for failure. Most people are afraid of failing, afraid of making a mistake, afraid of screwing up. Fear prevents them from taking the risks necessary to succeed. But success starts at the beginning. All successful people started as beginners in their fields of expertise.

A beginner is not merely a person who lacks knowledge. Beginners are more than the knowledge they do or do not possess. A beginner is someone new to a process or experience, someone embarking on a new journey. Beginners are willing to try something that they've never done before, such as traveling across the United States or running in a marathon. They are new to a particular experience, and therefore they have not yet developed the skills of someone who has done something numerous times. Beginners may also be associated with chronological age. It is assumed that if you are young, you must be a beginner.

For the purpose of this book, a beginner is simply defined as a person who has little or no experience with the concept of abundance. Whether you are twenty-two or eighty-two, you are a beginner at understanding and creating abundance. As with most things in life, it is important to start at the beginning. Beginnings are important; they create a strong foundation for whatever is about to come. Beginnings allow you to prepare, and to acquire the knowledge and know-how necessary to accomplish great things.

The first step on your path to plenty is to give yourself permission to be a beginner. In all areas of life, you start out as a beginner. You were a beginner when you were learning the alphabet and your math facts. You were a beginner when you learned to ride a two-wheel bicycle. You were a beginner when you started your first job. It is all right to be a beginner. Being a beginner does not mean that you are unintelligent; it just means that you are learning.

The world is full of experiences that you have yet to try. Indulge yourself in the new. It is there that you will discover your likes and dislikes, your abilities and your weaknesses. Life is the teacher and you are the new student in a large classroom. It is time to learn something new. Embrace new beginnings! After all, there will always be something new to explore, discover, and experience in your life.

When you are looking at experiencing abundance, there is no better place to start than at the beginning. The beginner starts with a fresh perspective. Beginners are excited and enthusiastic about that which will happen. Beginners are eager to learn and to apply their acquired knowledge in creative ways. Eagerness and enthusiasm are key ingredients to creating a life of profusion.

Think about other experiences that you've had as a beginner. Were you a beginner dancer or guitar player? Were you a beginner in art or theater? You have already had many experiences as a beginner. What did it feel like to be a beginner? Were you embarrassed? Did you feel unwise? Were you eager to find answers or did you avoid asking questions? How did you handle being a beginner? Examine the positive feelings of being a beginner.

Beginners are often treated differently from those with advanced skills. For instance, when you were learning to drive a car, others were more cautious or more forgiving of your driving abilities. The student driver gets special acknowledgement. As an identified beginner, you may be given privileges that others who "should know better" don't receive. It is as if others give you permission to learn by making mistakes—a sense of permission that this culture otherwise lacks.

If you are a beginner and something bad happens, it is perceived with understanding or compassion: "He's just learning." If you are a beginner and good things happen, others perceive it as beginner's luck. For instance, let's say that your uncle teaches you how to play poker and you win the first three hands of the game. How did that happen? People can only explain your win as luck, since you are new to playing the game. The first time you succeed at something new and unfamiliar, your success is considered to be beginner's luck.

Although beginner's luck is nice to experience, it is only temporary. Luck doesn't last indefinitely; it's finite. That is, you might not be lucky the next time you play poker. Luck is random. A desired result occurs by chance; it doesn't involve skill or strategy. There are people who win the lottery, acquire a great deal of money and material possessions, and eventually lose most of their fortune. Their good fortune came and went; these people were unable to maintain the presence of good fortune in their lives. This is the difference between luck and abundance. Abundance surpasses anything you can achieve due to luck.

Young and old alike buy into the philosophy that wealth and prosperity require luck. Is luck the only way to experience great quantity? Could you be without luck and live in abundance? Why not? There are people who do. Abundance doesn't know how lucky or unlucky you are.

Abundance is typically associated with the rich: it is supposedly the wealthy and prosperous people who have abundance, who have "more than they know what to do with." It is assumed that such people can have whatever they want. They can do what they want because "they have the money." Others perceive them as living well, with nice homes and vehicles, and vacations to faraway places like Fiji. Abundance is typically equated with money and wealth.

Abundance seems like more than the average person can imagine: *How do they do that? What is their secret?* Most people want more material possessions than they currently have. They are curious, if not envious, of the lives that the rich and famous lead. They wonder what it would be like to have such abundance.

> *Congratulations! You have just won a wonderful and abundant lifestyle! What will you do now? Where will you live? Who will you live with? What kind of car will you drive? Many choices are now within your reach. You now have the ability to create your life just the way you want it.*

Can you imagine waking up one morning and being told that you had won not the car of your dreams, but the *life* of your dreams? Everything that you had dreamed of and desired would now be yours for the taking! Where is the entry form?

That is the dream that motivates people to succeed. Although you may be new to abundance, you will certainly join many other people who share your desire to experience a rich and abundant life. State lotteries are thriving as a result of people investing in the promise of a dollar and a dream. Do you play the lottery or purchase instant-win tickets? Do you hope to strike it rich one day? If so, you are one of the many millions of people who desire abundance. However, most people lack the know-how to have and enjoy abundance. If you had more money than you could count, what would you like to have in your life?

Most people yearn for more in life, but they rarely include the word "abundance" in their everyday vocabulary. You may want a nicer car, a better job, or multiple family vacations. Why not if you can afford it financially? Why not give yourself what you desire? There would be little reason not to have what you want in life.

Your dreams are unfolding in front of you, and you are about to merge with the world. There is much to look forward to and many dreams and desires to fulfill.

Perhaps you want to share your life with someone in a loving, respectful relationship. Maybe you want a nicer home. Or you hope to have children, either now or in the future. Almost certainly you want an ideal career that pays well and offers you a comfortable lifestyle. You want to do life right, and you don't want to make the same mistakes others have made. You want to venture out into the world demonstrating your own abilities, and you are eager to show others what you can do. If you are stepping out on your own path, why not allow abundance to be a part of the path?

What is abundance?

Webster's Deluxe Unabridged Dictionary defines abundance as "great plenty; an overflowing quantity; ample sufficiency." Most people associate abundance with money, but abundance is more than money. It is a lifestyle. Abundance is having what you want in life, and plenty of it. It means that you can have what you desire—a nice vehicle, a formal education, or a summer to travel abroad.

Do you spend a great deal of emotional energy worrying about finances? If you had what you needed, would you continue to worry? Abundance is an attitude. It is knowing that you have all that you need. If you believed that everything would turn out well, could you surrender your worry? Abundance is knowing that your needs will always be met.

Abundance is having more than you could possibly count. Abundance can include time, money, experiences, joy, happiness, security, fulfillment, and more. Abundance may include the following:

- Peace of mind
- Time to do what you want
- Working at what you love
- Time with family and friends
- Having what you need
- Manifesting with ease
- Freedom from worry
- Enjoying what you have
- Time to yourself
- Feeling grateful

- Feeling good about yourself
- Feeling good about life

People have different definitions of abundance, depending on their desires and previous life experiences. They may simply define abundance as having enough money to pay their bills. Previous generations did not often use the word abundance. Most people had "enough to live on." People in these generations were raised to believe in limitation, and therefore would have felt uncomfortable with abundance. Abundance speaks to having more than enough to live on.

Abundance is having what you desire in life. Abundance means having good things and good experiences. Abundance is freedom. Abundance is joy. Abundance is contentment. Life is filled with abundance—more than you could need, more than you could use, more than you could want. Abundance is about experiencing all the good in life.

Abundance is your birthright. The fact that you are a person who exists on this planet is an invitation to live in abundance. Abundance is a basic right. All of life exists in abundance. Take a look around. Notice the trees, the sky, the grass, the mountains, the lakes, the oceans, and the raindrops.

All of life exists in abundance, yet most people ignore this fact. They think that abundance is limited. They think that abundance exists for other people, but not for them. Yet abundance already surrounds you! The signs are all around you. There are numerous leaves and branches on every tree. The blades of grass and the stars in the sky are too many to count. Nature is a constant reminder of your right to abundance. Take a look around you!

Abundance is possible. However, it is not likely to happen to you in the way you may think. Although some people win the lottery and assume a fortune, most people play the lottery without winning. If you read the back of a lottery ticket, you will be astounded by the miniscule odds. Your chances of waking up to a pot of gold are very small.

Your parents were right. You must work for your success and abundance, and you cannot sit idly by waiting for it to happen. Don't wait for someone to pass away in order to live prosperously. True prosperity comes on your own dollar, not dollars that were earned by someone else.

It is not likely that anyone is going to simply hand you keys to your good fortune—to your ideal house, car, or life. It's for *you* to create. Like a potter who uses simple clay to create a masterpiece, you can use simple strategies for creating the life you want. You can begin today to build an abundant life for yourself. Abundance is something that you attract rather than something that you are born into. Therefore, abundance is possible for everyone who wants it. True abundance goes beyond beginner's luck. You sit at the hub of your own wheel of fortune. Learn how to create abundance in your life. Become a magnet for good fortune and abundance. Why wait until later? Now is the right time. Begin your life on the path of abundance. It's as easy as 1 . . . 2 . . . 3 . . .

1. Start with a solid foundation.

   I have a right to abundance.

2. Know that abundance already exists.

   I am surrounded by abundance.

3. Know that abundance is possible.

   I live in abundance.

What does it mean to be a beginner to abundance? It means that although you know what abundance *could be*, you have yet to learn how to manifest it. You are a beginner seeking the information necessary to experience abundance in your life. You now know that abundance has nothing to do with luck. Don't worry. You can still be lucky. You just don't need to depend on luck to live the life of your dreams. Abundance is a way of life that *you* create. The subsequent chapters in this book will provide you with the basic knowledge you need to create abundance.

The red carpet is rolling out in front of you. Step onto it and move toward your abundance. There is no need to run through the process, only to risk a fall. Move at a comfortable pace for learning and living. Finally, you don't need a wish for good luck; you simply need to enjoy the ride!

CHAPTER TWO

The Spirit within Abundance

All I have seen teaches me to trust the Creator
for all I have not seen.

Ralph Waldo Emerson

Just as the mouse in a maze wonders where he is and how he will get to where he wants to go, you no doubt wonder how your abundant life will unfold. The mouse in the maze has limited vision. He can only see what lies directly in front of him. His focus is on how to get around the immediate wall, and is therefore unable to comprehend what lies beyond that point. Does this all sound familiar? Do you become preoccupied with what is immediately in front of you while ignoring the bigger picture?

As you embark on your journey to an abundant life, it is easy to become fixated on your immediate situation. What is the immediate wall in your life? Are you worried about your finances or concerned about a relationship? Are you struggling in your job? It's not enough to believe that your life will undoubtedly unfold; you want to know the specifics. What will happen? *How* will it happen? Will you marry and have children? Will you continue to live in your childhood town or will you move to another area? Will you have a successful career? There are many questions, and very few answers.

Perhaps that is why people visit fortunetellers and psychics. They want to know what is going to happen in their lives. Most importantly, they want to know that everything will be okay. They want to know in advance that everything will turn out wonderfully: *They lived happily ever after. The end.*

Like the maze holding the mouse, life consists of various obstacles, challenges, and limitations. As is true for the mouse, there are times when you no doubt feel stuck and confused. Which way should you go? Which way *could* you go? You look for a direction. You feel frustrated and overwhelmed at times. Isn't there an easier way? Do you have to knock into walls before arriving at your desired destination? The answer is no.

Of course most people do knock into walls. They take the long, and often hard, course in life. They endure many bumps and bruises. The good news is that, although knocking into walls is the most common way of maneuvering through life, it is not the only way.

What will make your life journey simpler?

Imagine if the mouse stuck behind the wall of the maze could climb a ladder to the top of the wall. How would this higher perspective simplify his journey? In climbing the ladder, he now has a bird's-eye view of the entire maze. The previous feeling of hopelessness is replaced with encouragement. The mouse can now see the possibility of success. He is able to develop a plan for moving quickly and easily through the maze. As a result, the mouse can spend less time worrying and more time planning.

Now, imagine that the maze is your life and that you are the mouse. The walls represent various situations in your life in which you feel stuck and unable to move forward. The walls are the obstacles that you don't know how to get around. Perhaps you were closed out of a particular college course, your car won't start, or your boss is upset with you. You respond with fear and uncertainty. What should you do? Although the walls provide some direction, there are only two ways to go. You can move forward or backward. Yet fear prevents you from making a decision and taking a step in either direction. Instead of moving, you convince yourself that you can't do something or that you don't know how to do it.

> *Obstacles are not there to defeat you,*
> *but rather to empower you.*

Obstacles often feel intimidating. It is typical to back away from them and hope that they will somehow be removed from your life course. However, like the maze, they also serve a purpose. What are the obstacles telling you? Why are you stuck? Are you ignoring important details? Are you afraid to move forward? Move beyond dwelling on the mere fact that there is a wall in front of you. Get moving. If you are the type of person who stagnates, take time to read the best-selling book *Who Moved My Cheese?* by Spencer Johnson. It is a delightful story that will aid you in exploring your approach to life. Acknowledge the existence of the walls in your life. Discover what they may represent.

The present and immediate wall in your life has various meanings and interpretations. For instance, it could represent your ability to utilize what is directly in front of you, something that people often neglect. People are programmed to look beyond that which is in front of them, and therefore they miss out on available information. Consequently, such people feel frustrated and unhappy with their current circumstances because they are trying to get somewhere else. They treat the current circumstances in their life as burdens or roadblocks that prevent them from moving on to the next experience. They feel victimized by life's circumstances instead of empowered. Every wall is then perceived as a stumbling block instead of a stepping stone.

The walls that serve as obstacles often represent something physical in nature. People spend valuable time and energy trying to resolve physical issues in life. They worry about money and how to pay their bills. They worry about what might happen or what might not happen. They have to put fuel in the car and pick up laundry detergent from the store. They feel irritated when they can't find their car keys and depressed when their partner breaks up with them. Those are all physical aspects of living: the elements of life that you can see, touch, and feel. But you limit yourself when you dwell only on the physical aspects of life. There are things beyond that wall to see and experience as well. Life is more than what you experience on a physical level.

Stretch beyond the physical.

We are made up of various parts: the physical (body), the emotional (feelings), the intellectual (mind), and the spiritual (soul). Although some of these elements are visible both to yourself and to others, there are parts of yourself that only you know exist. The soul is the spiritual essence of a person, a delicate part of who we all are. The soul can be vital, as it is in a person who practices spirituality on a consistent basis. The soul may also be dormant, as it is in a person who is unaware or who lacks knowledge of the existence of his or her soul.

Spirituality provides a higher perspective.

What if there were a way that you could have a bird's-eye view of your life as it unfolds? Imagine what it would feel like to know at the start that things were going to work out well. Could you then move forward with ease and peace of mind?

Spirituality moves you to a higher level and provides a broader perspective on the intricacies and details of life. You gain a global picture from a higher, more spiritual perspective. When searching for abundance, look around you. Look in front of you and look behind you. And then, finally, look up.

Many people feel intimidated by spirituality. They are reluctant to look up. They feel more comfortable with the physical: with what exists directly in front of them, that which they can see and touch. Spirituality is vague and ambiguous. It is not easily understood and there are various beliefs and interpretations. Consequently, spirituality poses a threat to some people, while others ignore or avoid it. Spirituality and religion are two terms that are commonly used interchangeably. They are similar, but they are also different.

Webster's Deluxe Unabridged Dictionary defines religion as the "belief in a divine or superhuman power or powers to be obeyed and worshipped as the creator(s) and ruler(s) of the universe; expression of this belief in conduct and ritual." Religion includes certain beliefs or practices that are shared by others of the same religion, typically including a place of worship such as a church or a synagogue. People seek love, acceptance, and community—and they often look to religion to fulfill those needs.

Some individuals perceive religion as severely authoritative, something to be avoided rather than embraced. These people believe that religion lacks, in practice, the compassion and unconditional acceptance that is described in many religious doctrines. Instead, they feel that religion emphasizes the belief that God is punitive and should be feared. For them, religion and spirituality part ways at this point.

Religion is the context and structure through which spirituality is observed and practiced. Most religions are governed by rules that are created and reinforced by the religion's adherents. Most people resent rules, particularly if they deem the rules to be unfair or unethical. They resist when others tell them what to do; they do not want to be told how to behave or what to believe.

Religion expects its followers to abide by the rules or else risk punishment or rejection. Although rules were developed to protect people, they can also alienate them. When individuals disagree with a rule, they separate themselves from the whole. They pull away in an effort to avoid feeling controlled or manipulated. They are fearful, and consequently can separate from religion as a means of protection. They cease to feel *a part* of the community and instead feel *apart* from it. They become a separate entity struggling with negative emotions.

If you feel alienated from a physical community, you will pull away from a spiritual connection. You may end up mistaking God's people for God. If you perceive a separation and rejection from God, it is likely due to how you were treated by other people. Fear and spirituality interlock. People think they fear God, when in fact they are afraid of the judgment and shaming of human beings.

You may have many reasons for avoiding organized religion. Religion is an external process that physically represents one's spirituality. Church attendees are typically perceived as "religious" for the simple reason that they practice a religion or visit church regularly.

It is assumed that religious people are closer to God, and so they are expected to behave in a God-like manner. But religious people are still humans with emotional insecurities. Someone who leaves church and is observed swearing at a pedestrian on the street is considered hypocritical. Religious people are perceived as hypocritical when they don't "practice what they preach."

Yet someone's actions and reactions to a situation align more with their perception of self (self-esteem) than with their spirituality. In other words, they are reacting from a place of fear rather than from a connection to the God-consciousness. They become frustrated with others because they are frustrated with themselves. In an effort to feel better, they criticize or condemn others.

Even religious clergy and those in authority are not immune from poor self-esteem, and therefore are not immune from inappropriate comments and gestures. They are people too, battling their past wounds and enduring insecurities.

Poor self-esteem is a precursor to judging others.

Judgments are inaccurate; they are simply a projection of insecurities onto someone else. Yet religious people are often perceived as severely judgmental of others, which contradicts most religious values. Thus, religion has sadly become taboo for many, instead of being a positive way to honor spirituality. Spirituality was meant to be honored, not feared.

Some people were spiritually abused in their past. Our society has only begun to understand the long-term effects of physical, emotional, and sexual abuse, and has yet to recognize the implications of spiritual abuse. Spiritual abuse is any abuse that is related to the development or experience of spirituality or religion. Anyone who was physically, sexually, or emotionally abused by someone affiliated with a religious order has experienced spiritual abuse. When abuse happens within a spiritual context, confusion occurs with regard to one's spiritual beliefs and spirituality is compromised.

Although many people were made to go to church as children, some of these people may not perceive their churchgoing as a forced ritual, but rather as a sincere part of their spiritual development. Other people who feel that religious practices were forced on them, and who therefore avoid such practices, were spiritually abused. Spirituality has been contaminated by forcefulness, and those abused therefore avoid rather than embrace spirituality. For them, trauma is associated with the experience of spirituality and religion, which continues to negatively affect the person to the point of avoidance.

Religion can leave people floundering in confusion, feeling unsure of what to believe or how to practice what they do believe. As a result, some people avoid any spiritual practice or belief. They don't participate in organized religion, and even avoid developing a spiritual awareness. Even those individuals who were fortunate to inherit a meaningful religious or spiritual belief system from their families may abandon spirituality sometime during adulthood. It is easy to lose your way when you feel uncertain about a topic that is often considered vague and controversial.

Spirituality is simply a belief in God or a Higher Power.

Spirituality begins with the idea that there is an energy or force greater than you, and that this greater spiritual source created you and continually guides and protects you. Just as there are founders of organizations and authors of books, there is a force that created you and all that surrounds you. This greater source takes many forms and has many names: Creator, Maker, Allah, God or Goddess, the Universe, Jesus, Jehovah, or Great Spirit. The most common name is God. However, the term "the Universe" is also commonly used since that term incorporates a general understanding of spirituality.

The Universe poses a challenge in that it is not present in a concrete physical form. You can't see the Universe in the way you might see an old friend in the supermarket aisle. The Universe is much greater than the physical world.

In this way, spirituality is difficult to understand, particularly for those without a spiritual history.

In the movie *Oh God!*, John Denver played the role of a simple man who is chosen by God (played by George Burns) to reveal His messages to the world. At first, Denver's character is overwhelmed. He questions why God would choose him when there are more religious people from whom to choose. He cannot understand why he has inherited a responsibility for something he knows little about: God. Denver's character fears that other people will think he is insane.

Judgment impacts spirituality.

We live in a severely judgmental society. Human nature seems to invite judgment as an acceptable part of our personal makeup. Few people are exempt from the tendency to judge others, and judgment makes it difficult for us to feel comfortable with religion and spirituality. Worrying about what others might think invites doubt about the presence of God in our daily lives. We further question the concepts of spirituality and religion. There are various denominations of religions and just as many churches, synagogues, and mosques that serve as places to worship. But what does it all mean? More importantly, what does religion have to do with abundance?

There is a spirit within abundance that deserves acknowledgement. It is necessary to recognize God or the Universe as the source of your abundance. Abundance is a spiritual concept. It has less to do with what you own and more to do with your spiritual connection. We are not meant to journey through life alone. There are guides to direct us and guideposts to light our way. Our job is simply to open up to this knowledge and to utilize its guidance.

Abundance is a gift from the Universe. All good comes from the Universe. As a result, it is necessary to develop a spiritual connection that will grant you the riches of the kingdom. Perhaps you already have a spiritual connection, a knowledge base of spirituality that you inherited from your family. If so, you may need only to fine-tune your understanding and use this most powerful influence. What do you believe in? Think about your own family history of spirituality. Are there values and beliefs you inhereted from your family that still exist within you? Do you believe in God? Do you call on God in times of need?

Religion is not perfect and it is not likely to become perfect soon. Although you may be interested in a particular religious demonination, you may also disagree with some of its beliefs. Religious teachings are filtered through human interpretation, and you may find it necessary to experience several religious groups before you find one that feels comfortable.

Still, some people within the organization you choose may come across as harsh, and so you may be at risk for judging the group you choose because of its people. Keep in mind that a church is less about its people and more about honoring a relationship with God. Choose spiritual beliefs and practices that strengthen your relationship with your spiritual connection. There is a spiritual energy that surrounds and lives within each of us. Plug yourself into the current that is already there.

What could you believe in? Sometimes it will be necessary to customize your spirituality based on your beliefs and personal practices. For instance, perhaps you connect more with nature than with a specific spiritual being. Maybe you connect with the oak tree in your yard. You are aware that this particular tree is special to you; there is an inexplicable connection between you and the tree. The oak tree can serve as the entry point of your developing spirituality.

Explore religions that are compatible with such connections. For instance, Native Americans have traditionally experienced spirituality through nature and animals. Choose a spiritual practice and understanding that feels comfortable to you, and take the time to research and discover your own interests that elaborate on your inherent beliefs. Customize your spirituality to reflect your relationship with the Universe. What is the most powerful way of connecting with this spiritual presence? Is it a particular church or is it a sweat lodge? Do you feel comfortable saying familiar prayers or do you prefer to create your own way of communicating with the Universe? Do you prefer the solitude of meditation or the liveliness of a church community? What is the most powerful yet comfortable way for you to connect with the Universe? The exercise at the end of the chapter will provide you with an opportunity to begin your exploration of spirituality.

Meditation is an effective way to get clarity while improving your overall health. How is that possible? Meditation cultivates stillness. We live in a restless society that encourages busy action rather than stillness. Most people expect that others will be busy and stay busy.

By incorporating a spiritual practice, such as meditation, you can explore the depths of abundance. Spirituality is a unique looking glass that enables you to see things clearly, albeit differently. You can see not only one tree but a forest of trees. With closer examination, your understanding deepens and you observe more than a single isolated tree. You can now recognize its underlying meaning of support and shelter. Your focus shifts and you recognize that you are not alone. You have reached a spiritual understanding from the existence of one simple tree.

As you look beyond the physical and into the spiritual, you will touch the magic—and experience more than you ever imagined. Life is abundant, if only you can see and experience it as abundance. A spiritual view of life is more expansive than the physical view of life. There are no limits. *With God all things are possible.*

When you believe in God, all lack and limitation transform into extraordinary opportunities. For example, imagine that you feel disappointed when you find out that a job you wanted was filled by another candidate. But yet in time you go on to find a different job with a larger salary and more flexibility.

Be mindful that when a window appears to close, it is time to watch for a door to open. God is everywhere and in everything. You are a part of this universal connection, and you are therefore always provided for in ways that you never imagined. God and abundance are interchangeable. You cannot have one without the other.

Everything in life is sacred, touched by God. Discover the sacred in all that you see, touch, smell, hear, and experience. Spirituality will then no longer be a weekly church visit, but rather an everyday experience. You look around and experience the hands of God in your life. Adopt the following universal spiritual beliefs as guideposts along your path to abundance:

There is a divine plan for your life.

Spirituality is a companion in life that allows life to unfold gracefully and without self-induced struggle and hardship. The Universe has a plan, a divine plan, for your life. Trust the Universe that your life is unfolding in exactly the right way. Don't fight the experiences in your life, which will only create unnecessary struggle. Let go and allow your life to be easily guided by the Universe. You are in good hands. Become flexible enough to move with the plan, even when the plan differs from your own. Choose to believe that everything is all right. You are okay. Your life is okay. You are being divinely guided.

There are no accidents.

The Universe does not make mistakes. It knows exactly what it is doing. The Universe is aware of what will move you to your greater purpose in life. It has the overall plan in hand. Your mission is to grow stronger, greater, more capable, and more spiritual on the journey. Although it may be necessary to confront challenges along the way, you are already guided in a way that achieves the mission.

Everything happens for a reason.

Trust in the Universe. If something is meant to happen, it will happen. Likewise, if something is not meant to happen, it will not happen. Life is purposeful. All experiences occur to serve a divine purpose for you on your journey toward wholeness and spiritual enlightenment.

Join forces with the CEO of your life and experience the ease with which your life unfolds. The Universe is the source of your abundance. Begin today to invite this most powerful and influential source into your life and see your dreams and desires materialize physically. What you once thought would never happen will happen with little effort.

Spirit is the invisible force behind the experiences in your life. There are experiences in life that are not easily explained; they have been touched by spirit. Open up to the existence of spirit in your life. Look. Listen. Feel. The Universe demonstrates its presence in the sky, through the clouds and through rays of sunshine. The Universe is in the wind and in the falling rain. The Universe speaks to you in the thunder and lightning. It reveals to you its generous nature in the abundance of trees and in the beauty of sunsets. The Universe sends its messages through songs on the radio or in conversations you have with other people. See and experience the Universe's presence in your daily life. You and your life are in good hands.

Spirituality.

My personal definition of spirituality is:

_____

_____

_____

_____

_____

_____

_____

I grew up being told:

_____

_____

_____

_____

At this time in my life, I believe:

_____

_____

_____

_____

I call my spiritual connection:

_____

I would like to develop my spirituality by:

_____

_____

_____

_____

CHAPTER THREE

Stepping on the Path to Abundance

To accomplish great things, we must not only act but also dream, not only plan but also believe.

Anatole France

Now that you have recruited the ultimate source of your abundance, it is time to establish your path to abundance. Consider for a moment what you want your path to abundance to look like. Close your eyes and picture your ideal path. Is it a dirt road, with protruding rocks? Is it a paved road, smooth but narrow? Is it a stone path? Is it a natural path of grass or shredded bark? Is it a path of bricks or limestone? This is the time to create your personal vision of your path to abundance. Allow it to develop in your mind, just as you desire it. Doing so is the first step toward stepping onto the path of abundance.

Perhaps your path is colorful or shining brightly, as if it were made of diamonds. Your path represents what you wish to create as you move forward in your life, claiming what is rightfully yours: abundance. Tuck that image of the ideal path to abundance safely inside your heart. In this way, you will be able to revisit your image time and time again.

Your path to abundance begins when you make a choice. It is as if there is already a fork in the road, and you must now choose between two roads with opposing directions. But which road will you choose? Is one road brighter and more revealing than the other? Does one path offer you a promise that the other path doesn't seem to hold? Abundance is as simple as making a choice. Yet some people torture themselves before making even the simplest of choices. The fear of making a mistake or making a "wrong choice" complicates the matter further and delays the process. People fear that they will regret the choices they make for a long time afterward.

Some people avoid making choices in their life, and would prefer to "take what they can" rather than risk making a mistake. They forfeit their right to make a choice. Their lives consist of decisions made by default, and they take whatever is left over after others make their choices. They are rarely the first in line. Instead, they wait to see if there will even be a space for them in line. Why do people approach their life in such a way?

Human beings struggle with making decisions for a variety of reasons. They often feel afraid, whether that fear is at a conscious or an unconscious level. Fear is the predominant factor affecting decision-making ability. Indecisive people may fear other people's perception of them. They are afraid of being judged, and they lack the positive self-esteem that would allow them to take their rightful position in life.

Poor self-esteem will lead you to feel inferior to others, and consequently less important and less capable than they are. People with poor self-esteem perceive themselves as not good enough and feel inadequate. If you lack self-esteem, you are likely to surrender your beliefs and adopt the beliefs of someone else. The truth is that whenever you compare yourself to another person, you will always end up feeling inferior. These are the familiar but unconscious feelings of shame and unworthiness.

If you do not believe in yourself, you will become dependent on the opinions or decisions of others. You will be vulnerable and your dreams and aspirations will be vulnerable.

When making choices and decisions in life, you must believe in yourself. You must trust yourself to make a good choice. If you struggle with making decisions, begin today to work toward trusting your decisions. Make little decisions, but make decisions nonetheless. Avoid responding to others with answers such as "I don't know" or, worse yet, "I don't care." Force yourself to make decisions, regardless of the subject matter or the impact of those decisions.

Avoid asking others what they think. People dining together commonly ask each other questions such as, "What are you having?" But have you noticed how the answer to that question influences your choice? If the other person tells you that they're having a sandwich, you may change your mind from the dinner meal you were considering and order a sandwich instead. It is human nature to want things to be equal and the same. But regardless of how strong your self-esteem is, try to avoid allowing others to influence your decisions. Believe in yourself and your decisions. After all, your decisions matter most.

You decide the path of your life. There are at least two types of paths to your abundance. The first path is the path most frequently traveled. There is visible evidence of those who have traveled it before you. It seems promising, only because you know that others have chosen it also. This is the familiar path through life. It represents what you know and what you have seen others experience and achieve. Yet this familiar path is the path of struggle. Although it is familiar, it is a challenging path consisting of rough terrain with various twists and turns. It is chosen on the basis of being familiar. If you look carefully, there is another path.

This other path to abundance appears simple and straight at first glance, but you wonder if it truly is. After all, it is not the path that other people most readily choose and travel down. Instead, it appears neglected and deserted. This is the path that represents the unknown, unfamiliar, and unexplored route through life. It may mean taking a different career route or simply working for a paycheck. This path will require you to think and act differently from other people.

The unknown is merely a lack of knowledge about the future. As such, it is not enough to stop events from happening. Life consists of unfolding experiences, most of which are not yet known to you. Acknowledge your fear of the unknown and begin to move forward.

Allow life to unfold in front of you, even though you are uncertain about what will happen.

The fear of the unknown can prevent you from moving forward on your chosen path to abundance. Yet most of life begins as an unknown. Life consists of one unknown followed by another. Tomorrow is unknown. Next year is unknown. Your future is unknown. No one knows what, when, or how anything will happen.

Avoid making decisions based solely on the fact that others have made those same decisions. Learn to make your own decisions. You know what is best for you. Choose the path of least struggle and resistance. Make things easy on yourself. Ask yourself the question "What is the easiest way to do this?" By answering that question, you will choose the easier path through life. Allow this important question to be an integral part of your decision-making process. What could your easy path to abundance look like?

Abundance is living life fully.

Abundance is attracted to ease, not to struggle. Unfortunately, most people have been led to believe otherwise, that life consists of pain and struggle. We are taught that what we desire comes only from working extremely hard, and that we must work long hours to have what we want. Our society is made up of people who work all the time. Most people are too busy to enjoy life. They are on the fast track, working longer and harder to accumulate things that they will not have the time to enjoy. Although you can accumulate wealth in this way, abundance is more than wealth. Abundance goes beyond simply working to accumulate money and material possessions. Abundance is the enjoyment of life.

As a beginner to abundance, you must adopt the attitude of abundance. Abundance is a lifestyle of ease and not of struggle. Choose to approach life tasks with ease. It is not necessary or beneficial to struggle. Life was not meant to be complicated or to provoke fear. Your path of abundance is easy.

"What is the easiest way of doing this?"

As you move forward with ease on your path to abundance, give yourself permission to dream. Do not limit yourself by what you think you can have in life. Permit yourself to be open to all the possibilities. Write your own permission slip to have what you desire in life:

Dear_____[family/friends/co-workers/world]:

I fully give my permission for _____[name] to have what he/she truly desires in life. After all, he/she deserves it!

Signature

_____

We do not have to wait for others to give us permission to move toward our dreams and desires. Each of us is the creator of our own dreams, and we must give ourselves permission to move in the direction of their fruition. Millions of people surrender their dreams while waiting for others, such as parents and mentors, to grant them permission. Do not wait for someone else to tell you that you would be a great actor, singer, or lawyer. Give yourself permission to advance toward your own dreams.

Now that you have permission, what is it that you desire in your life? What do you want to do with your life? Which experiences are you looking for? Allow yourself to dream without limitation. If you were presented with a catalog of life experiences, which ones might you choose?

Complete the Desires Checklist at the end of this chapter to align your thinking with your dreams. That checklist is in no way a complete list. Some people know what they want in life, but struggle to give themselves permission to move forward. If you are a person who truly does not know what you desire in life, the checklist will help you to begin the process.

It is important to know what you want in life. Move toward your desires, rather than heading toward something that will "do for now." Set your course from the beginning in the direction you want to move. Don't waste time and energy settling for less than what you desire, only to have to backtrack later and start again.

But despite what you may believe, or what others may tell you, you do not need to know *exactly* what you desire. Life is rarely an absolute, particularly when you are beginning on the path of abundance. Be willing to experiment and experience. Develop your ideas. Try new things that interest you. Always move in the direction of your interests. In doing so, you will still be moving forward on your path rather than sitting idly, waiting to make a decision.

Everyone has desires, but few people are courageous enough to fulfill them. Take the time to formulate your desires. Permit yourself to dream. Imagine what it would be like to have what you desire. Life is a canvas on which we create what we want. Be open to any and all possibilities. It is okay to have what you want! In later chapters, you will discover the tools for manifesting your dreams.

Your path is unfolding before you.

What do you want to have on your path to abundance? What would an abundant life look like to you? Would it be rich with money and material possessions? Would it be full of experiences and opportunities? Take a moment to close your eyes and imagine your abundant life. Imagine what it looks like and feels like. If you are a visual person, you are likely to see images. If you are not a visual person, you can use a different sense, such as touch or smell, to imagine your abundant life. There isn't a right way or a wrong way to do this exercise. Simply give yourself permission to imagine, and to see, feel, and experience whatever emerges. Record any observations in a journal or notebook.

Your path to abundance must include your true desires.

Refrain from filling your life with people, places, and things that do not represent your desires. That can easily happen, and it has happened to many others. Life, when not directed, still happens. As opportunities arise, refer to your completed Desires Checklist at the end of this chapter. In doing so, you won't be as likely to settle for less than what you truly desire.

When looking for a relationship, refer to those characteristics you checked in the spouse/partner section of the Desires Checklist. People who lack self-esteem generally choose to take what comes rather than to wait for what they truly desire. They are often afraid of living life alone, without a relationship, so they settle for whoever comes into their lives. They settle for who chooses them, rather than for whom they choose.

> *Success in life depends on your willingness*
> *to take chances.*

Do not allow fear to choose whom you date, no less your life partner. Choose your partner on the basis of love, not fear. Fear rears its ugly face in most areas of life. People become fearful that they won't have what they need, and they convince themselves that settling is better than nothing. They end up settling for less than they deserve.

Such people might get a job for the primary purpose of earning a paycheck. The paycheck is the reason they work. They become unwilling to risk losing their paychecks, and so they stay stuck in a particular job or company for many years. As the clock continues to move forward, they find it more difficult to leave their jobs even when they feel unhappy or unfulfilled. As they accumulate years of service, their salary and benefits increase and they feel stuck and unable to leave. Consequently, they begin to entertain ideas of retirement: *When I retire, I will . . .* But now they have to wait for more time to pass in order to live an abundant and enjoyable life.

As a beginner on the path to abundance, be aware of this trap and do not fall victim to this societal norm. If you have to change jobs frequently on your way to abundance, do so; it will still be better than sacrificing your life for a paycheck. Take chances. Success in life depends on your willingness to take chances. Take a chance at choosing work that you enjoy doing. Don't allow the judgments of others to contaminate your life. People are quick to judge, and if you choose to change jobs more than once, others may judge you. But don't allow the insecurities of other people to lead you off the path of abundance.

Remember: this is your life. You must decide what is best for you. Take the time necessary to discover your ideal work. Your ideal work will be one that stirs a passion within you. It will often be the kind of work that comes naturally to you. Again, abundance is ease and not struggle. Your ideal work will be exciting and enjoyable. The money earned is an additional benefit, as you will feel content doing what you love. Use the Ideal Work Meditation in appendix B of this book to get an idea of your ideal work.

Home is a common area of abundance for many people. Perhaps you dream about your ideal home more readily than about your ideal relationship or career. It is acceptable to dream about having, buying, or building a home, and it feels comfortable to tell others about your dream home. Some people have vague ideas about their ideal homes while others have concrete plans. Do you have a vision of your ideal home? Do you tell others that you have always wanted to live in a log cabin-style house or another specific type of home?

Manifesting your ideal home.

Unfortunately, the ability to describe your desires to someone else is not enough to manifest those desires. You will learn more about this tool in later chapters. Imagining your ideal home is simply another area in which you need to give yourself permission to dream. You deserve to have what you desire, including a nice place to live.

When looking for a place to call home, be selective. Don't choose a home based merely on what you can or cannot afford, as many people do. Don't settle for financial reasons, only to regret it later: *Well, that's all we could afford at the time.* Decisions based on finances will cost you more later. You may be locked into your chosen home for many years. In fact, many people purchase what they think is a starter home, only to end up living in the same house for dozens of years.

Again, your life is unfolding. It may not be easy to make the changes later that you are planning today. If you are considering buying a starter home, set a timeline to move to the home of your truest desires. Or establish goals for making this particular house more of what you truly want. You deserve to live in a house that you love, not simply one that you can afford at a given time. Perhaps you dream about building your own house, and about designing and planning that ideal home. Or you might prefer the simplicity of having all those decisions already made for you. Choose what is best for you. Your chosen home, whether temporary or permanent, will reveal something about your true self. Choose a home that you want and that you love.

If you settle for less than what you truly desire, you will always be enticed to want more. Abundance means feeling content and satisfied. Do not settle for anything less than what fully satisfies you.

You deserve to have what you desire.

Review the spiritual concepts of the previous chapter. There is a divine plan for your life. Remember that nothing happens by accident and that all things happen for a reason. These are the principles of abundance that will guide you on your path.

There is no longer any need to settle. Keep moving. Your desired good—whether it is a relationship, a career, or an ideal home—is on its way. Be patient and keep moving in the direction of your desires. When you settle for less than what you truly want, you walk off the path of abundance and abandon your dreams and desires. You settle for what you think you can have rather than moving forward toward what is possible. You take a detour. This detour may or may not include struggle, but it will cost you valuable "life time." Your arrival at your desires will be delayed indefinitely during your detour. In the worst-case scenario, you will walk off the path and never choose to get back on it. You will have settled for a life that is merely "good enough."

Most people live lives that are just good enough. They settle, while always wondering if, and hoping that, they will someday have what they really desire. You deserve a life that is more than just good enough. You deserve abundance. The abundant life means having what you want, and plenty of it. Don't walk off your path and settle for less than you desire. The path of abundance requires courage and discipline. Have the courage to move in the direction of your desires. Discipline will keep you on the path. Remind yourself periodically about what you sincerely want to have and experience in your chosen life. Keep your dreams in front of you at all times. Don't settle for less.

Settle only for abundance!

Desires Checklist.

Family desires:

Please rate your desires as follows:

(1) Necessary

(2) Nice to have, but not necessary

(3) Not desired

Spouse/partner:

____	Humorous	____	Physically attractive
____	Thoughtful	____	Considerate
____	Romantic	____	Affectionate
____	Hardworking	____	Strong communication skills
____	Self-employed	____	Playful
____	Friendly	____	Financially responsible
____	Family-oriented	____	Financially secure
____	Energetic	____	Emotionally available
____	Goal-oriented	____	Dependable
____	Reliable	____	Flexible
____	Hobbies/interests: _____		
____	Other_____		

Children:

____	None	____	Biological
____	One	____	Adopted
____	Two	____	Foster care
____	Three	____	Public education
____	Four	____	Private education
____	Five or more	____	Female(s)
		____	Male(s)

Home desires:

Please rate your desires as follows:

(1) Necessary

(2) Nice to have, but not necessary

(3) Not desired

____	Country/rural	____	Acreage
____	City/urban	____	Convenience (to work, stores)
____	Split-level	____	Small
____	Ranch	____	Moderate
____	Cape Cod	____	Large
____	Two-story	____	1 bedroom
____	Three-story	____	2 bedrooms
____	Modular	____	3 bedrooms
____	Cedar	____	4+ bedrooms
____	Brick	____	1 bathroom
____	Log home	____	2 bathrooms
____	Pool	____	3 bathrooms
____	Basement	____	Garage
____	Finished	____	Pond
____	Den	____	Fireplace
____	Family room	____	Fenced yard
____	Deck	____	Porch
____	Flower garden	____	Vegetable garden
____	Basketball court	____	Tennis court
____	Shaded yard	____	Proximity to neighbors
____	Bar	____	Jacuzzi
____	Barn	____	Live in hometown
____	Other_____		

Work desires:

____	Outdoors	____	Intellectual
____	With computers	____	Office
____	Creative	____	With machinery
____	Community space	____	Physical
____	Helping people	____	Private space
____	Emotional	____	Supervising people
____	Work at home	____	Traditional work hours
____	Administrative	____	Large corporation
____	Salary ($____)	____	Small business
____	Employee	____	With people
____	Flexible hours	____	Variable work schedule
____	Self-employed	____	Nontraditional work hours

Maximum commute: ____ 20 min. or less
____ 30–55 min.   ____ 60 + min.

CHAPTER FOUR

Break Away from the Old and the Familiar

The biggest adventure you can ever take is to live the life of your dreams.

Oprah Winfrey

As you move forward on your path to abundance, you are likely to encounter an occasional obstacle. It is therefore necessary to identify and explore these potential obstacles to your abundance in an effort to avoid feeling frustrated and discouraged later. Know that obstacles are an important part of your journey. They are not meant to stop you in your tracks, as many people tend to believe. By adjusting your pace, obstacles remind you to pause. They provide you with the ability to move forward in a conscious and well-thought-out manner.

Since you are in a hurry, it is easy to rush when manifesting your dreams. Obstacles slow you down when necessary. They help you to assess where you are—and where you are going—with your life. Obstacles are intended to raise your awareness, not to compel you to surrender your dreams.

The path of abundance is a continual path. Abundance exists in the process of living life; it is not achieved only upon reaching your final destination. Every step along the way is an opportunity to manifest and live in abundance. At times, you may wander off the path, but be mindful not to throw in the white towel. Choose never to give up! Acknowledge the obstacles, but always move forward.

Pause . . . but move forward.

The most common obstacle that you are likely to encounter is your past. Many people believe that they aren't affected by the past, and they attempt to sever themselves and their lives from it. Perhaps you feel ashamed by what you did in the past, and so you want to get as far away from your past as possible. You may not want to think about the past or be reminded of it in any way. You could be fearful of reliving the past, particularly when it consists of negative and hurtful experiences and emotions. You may prefer to believe that the past and the present are separate entities, and that one has nothing to do with the other. If so, you only want to address your present situation and ignore the past. In other words, you hope to start over in life.

Your past affects your present.

Patterns emerge that originated in the past, whether in past experiences, past relationships, or in past familial generations. It is not enough to just tell yourself that you aren't going to be like your mother. Patterns exist on a subconscious level. You can say that you will not repeat a particular pattern—but just saying that is not enough. The pattern still repeats. Patterns must be broken at the subconscious level, as well as at the conscious level. Thus, you feel frustrated and bewildered when an issue does not get better even after you have sought counseling and made other attempts to change. It is necessary to dip below the surface to see what is really happening.

The way in which you deal—or do not deal—with your boss today has its origins somewhere in your past. For instance, imagine that you have an angry and emotionally volatile boss, and that you feel victimized by his emotions on a regular basis. You try to avoid him, but that doesn't always work. He wants to see you in his office. You anticipate that he will be in another bad mood, but his bad mood still has a way of taking you by surprise. You are determined to get your work done as quickly as possible so he won't yell at you. Yet he yells at you anyway. You perceive yourself as getting smaller and less significant while he grows larger and more significant. Notice how his emotions affect you, and how his angry feelings control your behavior. How is that possible?

> *Most of your reactions today are*
> *in some way related to your past.*

You are no doubt affected by the angry emotions of others, emotions that have their roots in the past. When you are negatively affected by another person's feelings, ask yourself the question "Who does the emotional person remind me of?" You will be surprised to realize that there is someone from your past who has influenced the underlying cause for your reaction. The question is whether or not you can independently access the emotional database located in your subconscious mind.

An emotionally familiar experience causes you to react in a way that is similar to how you reacted to someone or something in your past. In other words, the face of the person provoking the reaction has changed, but your reaction to the emotions remain the same. Are you reacting in a similar way as you did when a previous boss, a parent, or a sibling expressed anger? Is it really about your boss? Or is it about your past?

Most of your reactions today are in some way related to your past. From whom did you learn how to take things in stride? From whom did you learn how to be sarcastic or critical? People are creatures of habit, and therefore patterns create obstacles that are then used as unconscious reference points. Consider this example:

> *Jay had a temper. He would get angry easily, to the point of throwing an object across the room or hitting a wall. His unpredictable behavior scared his wife and children. Jay felt unable to control his anger, but he didn't know why. Eventually, Jay recognized the pattern: he would get angry with his wife whenever he came home from work and she wasn't there.*

Patterns can exist in layers. There are four common patterns that develop from your past. *Behavioral patterns* occur when you behave or act in the same way someone else in your past did. These patterns can also include the ways that you continue to act despite your efforts not to do so. *Emotional patterns* exist when you feel the same as you did in your past. *Cognitive patterns* exist when you think as you or someone else did in your past. *Social patterns* are present when you treat others the same as you did in your past.

Jay's reaction, as described above, is an example of a pattern that originated in the past, but that continues to contaminate the present. Jay's mother was rarely home when he was growing up: he came home to an empty and quiet house every day after school. He never knew when anyone else would come home. As a child, he felt scared and abandoned by his family, in particular by his mother. Jay's emotional pattern revolves around his unresolved feelings of fear and abandonment, which he holds at the subconscious level. He most likely isn't aware of this powerful emotional connection between his past and present. He learned from his past that women—beginning with his mother—may not be there when he comes home or when he needs them. So he continues to think in this way and to react severely to the simple fact that his wife is not home. This is a cognitive pattern.

The next level is a behavioral pattern exemplified by Jay's angry physical outburst. As a child, Jay observed his stepfather express anger by yelling, swearing, and throwing things, so Jay mistakenly learned to express anger in the same way. His wife and children are adversely—and in some ways permanently—affected by his behavior. They feel as if they're walking on eggshells, not knowing when Jay will get angry again. This is a social pattern, which most likely reflects how Jay and his family reacted to his stepfather's behavior.

Jay represents a common but inappropriate reactionary system that demonstrates how people respond in the present based on experiences from their past. Human beings typically react severely to current circumstances, even though the influence on their actions comes from the past. When you are courageous enough to examine your past, you become less volatile and less reactionary. Firecrackers are more harmful when they are kept in a closed container rather than in an open area. Similarly, your past is less damaging when it is opened and explored instead of concealed and forgotten. The past is not to be used as a weapon, but rather as a teacher. Permit your past to shed some light on your present life and circumstances. Choose to see and understand the whole picture, not just portions of it. You do not exist in isolation from other people, nor in isolation from your past experiences.

What have you learned about abundance from your past?

Patterns of the past influence your movement on the path to abundance. Familial patterns in particular can impose upon and affect your success in life. We can fall prey to the beliefs of our parents or grandparents when deciding our future plans. If your family has certain negative opinions about a particular career that interests you, you might abandon that desired career. Artists who are told by others that they will starve become less passionate about pursuing a career in art.

Most people don't volunteer to starve. As a result, they base life-changing decisions on the opinions of others. We live in a fear-based society, and people's opinions often reflect their fears. Everyone is afraid of something or someone, and yet we're reluctant to acknowledge our fears. We pass our fears on in a socially acceptable manner, also known as offering opinions.

Fear is the predominant emotion that sits at the base of other feelings such as anger and hurt. It is not socially permissible to say "I'm afraid." Society views fear as a weakness. Most people are more comfortable admitting to feelings of hurt or anger than they are admitting to fear. Yet they tell other people what they should or shouldn't do, based on their own fears: "You don't want to be a doctor; they work all the time." In other words: "I am afraid that if you become a doctor you will be overworked and unhappy."

As members of a fear-based society, people judge others in order to relieve their fears. Individuals don't like to be judged by others and often feel unfairly judged themselves. Judgment is simply fear projected onto someone else. You may feel afraid of what others think and therefore pattern your life in a way to avoid the harsh judgments of others. You may choose a career or life path that others favor. There is a fine line between an opinion and a judgment. In fact, the two are difficult to separate most of the time.

You are vulnerable to the opinions of others when you doubt yourself and your abilities. A lack of self-esteem can lead you to believe that you are wrong and that they are right. And sadly, it does not matter who *they* are. *They* can include your parents, grandparents, siblings, neighbors, or close friends. You end up feeling inferior to the knowledge and abilities of others, and you end up doing what others expect you to do rather than what *you* want to do.

Imagine that your beloved grandparents tell you, "We need a lawyer in the family. You'd be a good lawyer." You do not want to disappoint your grandparents, so you convince yourself that your elders know better, given the wisdom of their advanced age and life experience. Consequently, the opinions of your grandparents weigh more heavily than your own opinions do.

Your needs as they conflict with the needs of others represent a battleground at times on the path to making your dreams a reality. You begin to base your decisions on what you *should* do rather than on what you *could* do.

Imagine that you take over your family's business because your parents think that is what is best for you. And it certainly could be, but is running the family business what you truly want to do? Or are you simply afraid of how your parents will feel if you don't assume the family business?

Know the difference between what *you* want and what others want for you. Sometimes the two are the same, but often they are not. Distinguish your needs from the needs and expectations of others by listening carefully to what you are thinking and saying. If the word *should* appears in your thoughts or words, you're probably following the expectations of someone else.

Should relates to an obligation. It implies that others expect you to do something and therefore that you *should* do it: *I* should *major in biology* or *I* should *stay in this job for the benefits*. Replace all *I should*s with the phrase *I would like to*. In doing so, you claim the intention as your own: *I would like to major in biology* or *I would like to stay in this job for the benefits*. It feels different—because it *is* different. Be true to yourself and to your desires. The opinions of others are simply the opinions of others.

Your dreams are yours to claim or to deny;
the choice is yours.

When you are charting new territory, the world can feel scary. You look for the support and reassurance of family members or close friends. As a result, such people often influence your desires and you look for their approval as you set out to create your life. In most cases, your family wants the best for you. They support your dreams and desires, and act as your personal cheerleaders. They cheer your progress and accomplishments from the sidelines. They encourage you to push through obstacles. Yet there are others who may discourage you or advise you to move in *their* desired direction. That is, they want you to achieve what they themselves could not achieve.

Every generation hopes to do better than the previous one. Some parents wanted a specific career or lifestyle for themselves, but they were unable to pursue their desires— and so they project their dreams onto their children. They push them toward computer programming or the Peace Corps. Ensure that you are pursuing *your* interests and not your family's unfulfilled dreams. Your parents mean well and want you to have more than they do or did. But there's a difference between encouragement and expectation. Your family needs to encourage you without expecting that you accomplish what they had hoped to accomplish.

Encouragement brings families together,
while expectations pull families apart.

Soliciting the advice of others is beneficial, as long as you hold true to your own genuine desires. Do not ask for advice from others if you doubt yourself; if you do so, you will be most at risk for surrendering your personal dreams and desires. Listen to the advice of others with discernment, but consider your own needs and desires first and foremost. If the advice you receive is consistent with your desires, you have been supported. If it isn't, then you need to determine what you need as opposed to what the other person may *think* you need. Perhaps your sister thinks that you would be good at electrical engineering. That is wonderful! But what do you think? Have you always been interested in electrical devices? Does it generate a passion in you? Would you enjoy that sort of work forty or more hours each week?

Listen to the opinions of others,
but make your own decisions.

You are also vulnerable to adopting beliefs as your own even though they originated with someone else. People in our families can and do impose certain beliefs on us, which is usually not a problem—unless we disagree with those beliefs. The problem is compounded when beliefs change. Imagine that you used to believe in the same things that other family members still do believe in, but that you have since adopted different beliefs. Families generally have a hard time with changes in beliefs. They may perceive your change in beliefs as a threat to the family belief system or, worse yet, they may feel abandoned by the change.

You probably have beliefs about everything in life, including religion, people, nutrition, politics, parenting, and more. Certain beliefs are often passed down through generations, much like holiday traditions. A similar philosophy within a family can create a feeling of safety and comfort: *We did it this way, and therefore you will do it this way.*

Of course, that is easier said than done. Sometimes, people forget that their families are actually comprised of individuals with distinct differences. None of us looks the same—yet some people think that all members of a family must believe in the same things and behave in the same ways.

Your inherited beliefs are those beliefs that you adopted from previous generations. You have no doubt inherited beliefs about family, time, money, abundance, and life. But do you know what those beliefs are? Most inherited beliefs are subconscious; they are not at the surface for your examination. You will need to drop down into your subconsciousness and examine the beliefs that are affecting your present and future.

What did you learn from your parents about money?

The exercise at the end of the chapter will aid you in exploring this important question. Although most people are afraid of not having enough money, there are people who are afraid to *have* money. The fear of not having enough money is self-explanatory: people are afraid of not having the money to pay their bills or to get what they need or want. When we fear not having enough money, we live with a feeling of lack and scarcity. We end up worrying about money, and are unsure of how we will pay our bills at the end of each month.

The fear of not having enough money affects many people, regardless of their incomes. People with large incomes also worry about money, and can experience the threat of lack and scarcity.

If you are afraid of *having* money, you might either hide your money or spend it. You may tell others that you don't have any money when the truth is that you have money that you choose not to spend. You cleverly disguise your money because you do not want anyone to know you have it. You are afraid that others will request a loan or, worse yet, that they'll steal from you.

You may feel ashamed to have money. Shame invites a spending pattern. You don't want others to treat you differently because you have money, and you don't want to be perceived negatively for having money. You may worry that others will judge you, or worry about what others will think if you have money or if you appear to have money. You might think that others will expect you to pay for things or to give away your money freely and generously.

Money is a part of the path to abundance. You need to explore your inherited beliefs about money in order to separate yourself from them. Otherwise, the pattern will repeat and you will experience money in the same way that your parents did.

Abundance means having enough money.

Although your opinion about money is an important inherited belief in your life, it is not the only such belief. You may have also inherited beliefs regarding time. People are afraid of not having enough time, and abundance also means having enough time.

Beliefs are typically associated with a person's value system. What values did your parents instill in you? Of those values, which remain important and worthy of continuation in your life?

The beliefs we inherited from our parents can and often do affect our life course. Such beliefs can cause people to live their lives for their parents or other loved ones, and not for themselves. Sometimes it is only much too late that such people wake up and realize this important fact. Life is not meant to be a power struggle, or an uprising of "you vs. them." Now is the time to separate yourself from any beliefs that are not truly yours.

Break away from beliefs that do not serve you or that used to serve you but that no longer do. It is possible to outgrow certain beliefs and to adopt new ones along life's path. Claim your life by claiming your beliefs. Be willing to accept that you may have beliefs that differ from those of other people.

Take responsibility for what you believe. You don't need to rebel in a defensive manner: there's a difference between being assertive and being aggressive. Holding true to your beliefs means being assertive, not aggressive. Beliefs do not have to be argued as right or wrong. They simply have to be believed by the person who holds them. Insecure people will argue their beliefs in order to prove to themselves that they are "right." Choose to avoid this pattern of behavior.

> *Honor your beliefs, while also acknowledging the beliefs of others.*

Breaking away from the expectations and patterns of others requires you to develop certain traits. First, you must develop and utilize effective communication methods. In other words, speak your truth, but do so in an empowering, not a defensive, manner. Tell others what you believe, and confront them in a non-aggressive way if they shame you or judge you. It is important that you feel worthy of your dreams and desires. After all, they will be difficult to achieve if you don't feel worthy of them.

You deserve a life that you love. Successfully breaking away means feeling comfortable about being independent. If you tend to rely on others, now is the time to practice independence. Take yourself out to the movies or to dinner. If you want to do something but no one is available, do it on your own. Develop your independence. Finally, your ability to break away depends on your feeling capable. Remind yourself daily, if necessary: *I am capable. I can do it.* Build up your sense of capability. It has most likely always been there; you've just never exercised it before.

The rewards of breaking away from the belief systems of others include better self-awareness, more self-confidence, and a greater sense of self-worth. When you recognize and understand your inherited beliefs, you are less likely to maintain them. Self-awareness allows you to know your beliefs and to differentiate them from the beliefs of others. Self-confidence provides you with the ability to assert your beliefs. Self-worth gives you full permission to hold your own beliefs, even when they are different from the beliefs of others.

Exercise

If there are certain beliefs others hold that continue to sabotage you or to hold you back from success, create a ritual of giving back that which is not yours and taking ownership of what is rightfully yours. Close your eyes and place a pillow on your lap. Put into the pillow all of the negative beliefs others hold that do not belong to you. Include them all and imagine them going into the pillow. Now, hand the pillow to an imaginary person who owns the beliefs. In a similar way, decide which beliefs are yours to take and reclaim them as your own. Positive thoughts can serve as affirmations. Reach your hand out and pull them into your heart. Complete this exercise with the statement "I believe in me."

Your success on the path of abundance depends on what you believe. You choose what you believe about yourself, about your life, and about your dreams. Choose to believe that all things are possible—and then observe how life unfolds before you.

What did you learn from your parents about money?

How did your mother view money?

_____

_____

_____

Was she a spender or a saver?

_____

Was she afraid of having or not having enough money?

_____

What were her rituals around money?

_____

_____

_____

How did her past contribute to this view and use of money?

_____

_____

_____

What did you learn about money from your mother?

_____

_____

_____

What beliefs did you inherit from her about money?

_____

_____

_____

Therefore, the belief I learned from my mother about money is: _____

How did your father view money?

_____

_____

_____

Was he a spender or a saver?

_____

Was he afraid of having or not having money?

_____

What were his rituals around money?

_____

_____

_____

How did his past contribute to this view and use of money?

_____

_____

_____

What did you learn about money from your father?

_____

_____

_____

What are the beliefs that you inherited from him with regard to money?

_____

_____

_____

Therefore, the belief I learned from my father about money is: _____

PART TWO

Abundance Is Easy:
The Nuts and Bolts
of Manifesting Desires

CHAPTER FIVE

Aligning Your Thoughts with Your Desires

Whether you think you can or think you can't, you're right.

Henry Ford

What are you thinking? Your mind is active, often overly active, with the constant motion of thoughts. Thoughts are continuous and come without effort; you are always thinking. You think when you have to think, such as when you are studying or solving problems at work. And you think even when you don't have to think—for example, before you fall asleep at night. Thoughts come when invited and thoughts come when uninvited. You think in the shower and while driving your car. Sometimes you don't mind such thoughts, while other times the thoughts disrupt your experience. You remain busy by thinking. Even when your body is idle, you can continue to busy yourself with thoughts. Thoughts serve a valuable purpose: you must think to know and think to solve problems.

But what are you thinking about? More importantly, *how* do you think? Do you think positively or negatively? In other words, are you an optimist or a pessimist? Do your thoughts reflect the bright side or the dark side of things? Do you perceive the famous psychological glass as half full or half empty?

Some people are natural optimists. Perhaps they were lucky enough to be born with a chromosome dedicated to optimism. They find it easy to see the bright and the positive sides of everything. They react differently from pessimists to life's disappointments. They do not get angry or frustrated, but appear instead to accept disappointing situations. When they don't get a job offer, they believe that something better will come along. When optimists lose a checkbook, they believe that it will eventually be returned. Optimists seem to always believe that good things will happen.

Some people were groomed to be optimists. They were taught from an early age to think positively; family members discouraged them from having negative thoughts. Children raised in an optimistic environment have an increased chance of becoming optimistic themselves. They learn to view life through a positive perspective. Optimists tend to live longer and are less likely to experience depression or anxiety.

How did your family influence your current thinking patterns? Were your parents optimists or pessimists? Were you encouraged to think positively? People who think negatively tend to be more critical of themselves and of others. Negative thought processes are typically reinforced by others. If your mother found your negative comments humorous, you probably became more likely to repeat the negative comments. When negative thinking is discouraged rather than encouraged, it eventually diminishes—and ceases to exist. Negative thinking is a drain on the energy of other people. It is hard to listen to after a period of time; it feels heavy and burdensome.

Other people seek the company of optimistic thinkers: they want to surround themselves with people who are light-hearted and fun to be around, and they are drawn to people at work and in the community who are optimistic. The positive attitudes of optimists add to the quality of others' lives.

Optimists also choose the company of other optimists. Those who want to be optimists choose such company in hopes of acquiring this positive energy. Optimism feels good.

The two thought processes, positive and negative, are opposing forces. They repel one another. Positive thinking is constructive thinking. It increases the likelihood of positive and desirable outcomes. Negative thinking, on the other hand, is destructive thinking. It has the power to produce undesirable outcomes. Negative thinking is the common pattern of thinking for most people. Catastrophic thinking, during which someone thinks the worst of a situation, is an intensified form of negative thinking.

What are you thinking?

It is difficult to pay continuous attention to your thoughts. Some thoughts are fleeting, while other thoughts seem to linger indefinitely. Disturbing thoughts grab your attention immediately, and frighten and alarm you. They force you to pay attention.

Typically, thoughts are negative but not alarming. Negative thoughts are enough to sabotage your path to abundance. You are aware of your negative thoughts at the conscious level, but there are negative thoughts at the subconscious level too, which escape your conscious awareness. You aren't aware of many of your negative thoughts—and yet they still exist. They still have the power to sabotage the manifestation of your desires.

Negative thoughts lie dormant, waiting for an opportunity for expression. People tend to think about the bad before they think about the good. Negative thoughts are on autopilot. You don't purposely steer your thoughts in a negative direction; it just happens.

Most people are programmed to think that bad things will happen before they think that good things will happen. They think that they won't get a promotion or that their car won't pass an inspection. Those events are certainly not what they want to have happen; it's just that they naturally think in a negative way. The truth is that most people—most likely, including you—think hundreds of negative thoughts every day, not to mention over the course of a life. Do not forget that your thoughts create your attitude.

Negative thoughts consist of fear and judgment. They reflect the old and neglected wounds of the past. Your negative thoughts are residual effects of the times when you felt disappointed or abandoned. Your thoughts follow your past experiences. As a result, you may think that you will fail an important test or lose a big game. You could think that your plane will be delayed or that your flight will be canceled. Fears underlie many of your thoughts, and negative thoughts communicate fear rather than hope.

Be aware of your thoughts and you will become aware of your fears. Are you afraid to fail or to succeed? Are you afraid of being alone or of making a mistake? Are you afraid of what others think of you? Fear lays the foundation for negative thoughts.

Most negative thoughts are fearful thoughts.

To dismiss your fear is to dismiss negative thoughts. Of course, that is not as simple as it seems. Most people compensate for their negative thoughts since they are unable to completely dismiss such thoughts. Instead, they find ways to avoid them.

Most people stay busy in an effort to control their negative thoughts: *I don't want to think about it.* They find something tangible to do instead. They balance their checkbooks, clean a closet, or run errands. They do whatever they can to avoid sitting still. Stillness invites thinking. No one wants to think bad thoughts about a particular situation or, worse yet, about their life, so people stay distracted by always having something to do. They can do more than one thing at any given time. They knit or read while watching television. They make sure that they always have work to do in order to keep their negative thoughts at bay. Avoidance works to some degree, but it also forces you to stay on guard against unexpected attacks of negative thoughts.

Negative thinking impedes abundance by creating obstacles on the path to abundance. Every fearful thought represents yet another obstacle. Consider how many negative thoughts you may have on any given day. How many obstacles to your abundance are you creating? If you think that things won't work out and that situations won't go as planned, then negative thinking will prompt you to prepare for disappointment. Perhaps you think that, if you prepare, the disappointment won't feel as bad. It still won't feel good, but at least it won't feel quite as badly as it would have without preparation. Maybe you'll tell yourself: *I knew that was going to happen.*

Many people are accustomed to thinking in terms of what they are afraid will happen: *I think I failed the test* or

I think I blew the job interview. The results are not even in yet, and such people are planning for failure and disappointment. Don't torture yourself prematurely with negative and fearful thoughts. Choose to think differently.

> ### Think only positive thoughts and
> ### expect only positive outcomes.

Thoughts are an illusion at best. That is, it is easy enough to *think* that something will happen even if it never does. Likewise, you can think that something *won't* happen even when it actually does.

Thoughts are unreliable. Acknowledge your thoughts without allowing them to consume your life. Thoughts are merely thoughts. Do not allow them to act as the authority over your life. Choose to think less. The mind is heavily burdened by thoughts, which can make you feel overwhelmed and confused. It is no wonder that millions of people suffer from headaches on a regular basis. They think too much! They have become intellectual nightmares. If you are always thinking and have a tendency to think the worst of a situation, you too have become an intellectual nightmare. Get out of your head!

Give your mind some needed time to rest. The level of stress that you experience has less to do with situations in your life and more to do with how you perceive those situations. It is your *thoughts* about a situation—and not the actual situation itself—that cause stress. In other words, when you think that you have a great deal to accomplish, you feel overwhelmed and stressed. No doubt you feel stressed before actually engaging in an activity, and the stress develops as a result of your thoughts. If you anticipate difficulty or hardship, you most likely think "I can't." And if you think that you can't do something, you aren't likely to put forth your greatest effort. Instead, you surrender to the negative thoughts.

Think less and feel more.

Thoughts distract you from your feelings. If you pull yourself into your thoughts, it becomes harder to feel. Our society is more comfortable with intellect than with emotion. People frequently ask others what they *think* about a situation before inquiring about how they *feel* about it. You can choose to think any way you want about any situation—and, in the end, all your thinking could still be meaningless. Your thoughts may be inaccurate. You can think long and hard about a big green monster sitting right outside your door. You can think about that monster so much that you feel scared to open the door. But it still does not mean that there is a monster outside the door. It simply means that you think there is one there and that you have convinced yourself to react to the mere thought.

Perhaps you think in this way on a regular basis, and you convince yourself that what you think is accurate even when it isn't. You may think, for example, that your significant other is attracted to someone else, even when there is no realistic basis for that thought. In point of fact, people often think in terms of what they fear the most.

Thoughts are easily confused with perception. Perception is based on how you see and experience situations. It is difficult to differentiate between thought and perception, as they are often grouped together. Yet perception has a greater rate of inaccuracy because it relies on personal interpretation. You customize your perception to meet your needs, something that is also true of your thoughts.

You choose your thoughts, so choose wisely!

Choose to think in ways that are conducive to your desires. Expand on the typical meaning of the saying "think what you will," and think as you intend. Think only about that which you actually want to happen. Ask yourself, "What do I want to have happen?" If you do so, you will move your thoughts in the direction of your desires.

Thoughts are unspoken intentions. Although your thoughts exist quietly within the recesses of your mind, they summon the attention of the Universe. What you think—and the ways in which you think—have a profound impact on your life path. Your thoughts are a direct line to the spiritual world, where dreams and desires regularly manifest. What you choose to think has the power and potential to manifest. Thoughts are energy. They put desires into motion.

Thoughts influence outcomes.

Your thoughts, despite dwelling inside of you, are powerful methods of communication. A seed planted in the ground cannot be seen, yet it still has the ability to grow into an enormous tree. Your thoughts are seeds. Good thoughts produce positive outcomes. Your chosen thoughts are influential in creating something extraordinary for your life. Plant only good thoughts.

If you are naturally optimistic, it will be easy to align your thoughts with your desires. If not, you must be vigilant with regard to your thoughts. Be alert and conscious of your thinking. Your thoughts must match your desires. If you want a promotion, think that you will get one. Do not get tangled up in the logistics, or surrender your potential promotion to negative thoughts such as, "There aren't any openings" or "No one ever leaves that department." Choose to believe that anything is possible. Think in terms of what you want to happen, not in terms of what *could* happen. Anything can happen. To think that there aren't any openings or that you won't get a promotion pushes the outcome toward that which you don't want to have happen. Think consciously. Think only in terms of your desires.

Think with conscious and careful consideration. Thoughts are powerful expressions of your intentions. If you think that something bad is going to happen, you increase the likelihood of something bad happening. Fearful thoughts produce fearful outcomes. Similarly, if you think in terms of what you want to experience, you are likely to attract what you desire. Thoughts are powerful! Think only in terms of your desires, and take careful note of what happens in your life.

Review your Desires Checklist from chapter 3 and relinquish any negative beliefs that you have about your desires. Do you believe that you will never meet a partner who shares your interests? Do you think that you won't get into medical school even though that is what you most want? Erase negative thoughts! Believe that all things are possible—and watch with amazement at what happens. Your thoughts bring your desires to fruition. Choose what you desire, and believe that what you desire is indeed possible for you to manifest and achieve.

Thoughts influence your present and your future. What you think could happen might indeed happen. Be mindful of your thoughts and correct negative or fearful thoughts. Negative thoughts don't serve you. You desire a life that is full of wonderful things and experiences. Entertain good thoughts.

Anticipate positive experiences and outcomes. Be creative. Entertain all of the possible positive outcomes that can emerge from a particular situation. Imagine that your roommate has decided to move in with her boyfriend. What will that mean for you? What are the potential *positive* outcomes of this situation? You may live alone for a period of time and find it rewarding. You may find another roommate who shares similar interests. Your boyfriend could move in with you. You could look for and find a cheaper apartment. Anticipate the good. No matter the situation, choose to think of the positive possibilities.

Negative thinkers can feel unworthy of their desires. They think that they can't have a college education or a dream home because they don't deserve such wonderful things, and they often feel jealous or resentful of anyone who has achieved their own dreams. Do not waste powerful thoughts on negative feelings, such as shame and unworthiness. Give yourself permission to have what you desire, and avoid punishing others for having what they desire. Remember, abundance is your birthright!

Choose to think in ways that serve you.

Change your thoughts and you will change your life. Remind yourself daily that you are worthy of all good things. Learn to receive from others without feeling guilt or shame. Receive all that is good and all that enhances your life. Receive gifts, kind gestures, and compliments. Say "thank you." Feelings of unworthiness impose guilt, which then demands that you pay others back or return the favor as soon as possible. Surrender your fear that other people will think badly of you or won't like you if things are not equal between you; it is not necessary that everything be equal. Allow people to demonstrate kindness to you. You deserve kindness. Open your arms and your life to receive. You are worthy of all good things in life.

Your thoughts are a powerful key that unlocks a life of abundance, so cultivate a positive way of thinking. Just as a silver coin has two sides, there are always two ways to think about a situation. Every negative thought has a positive counterpart. Find the positive side. When challenged with a situation, ask yourself: "What would be a *positive* way to look at this situation?"

Experience things for what they are rather than for what you think they are. Your thoughts will either aid you or prevent you from moving forward. If you think something bad is going to happen, you will stall. Or worse yet, you will stop in your tracks. Move forward and find the positive. As you search for the positive, it will become easier to find. You will soon discover that you don't need to look as hard as you did before. Positive thinking becomes effortless, something that is also true of abundance.

Abundance arrives with little effort.

Optimism will serve you well throughout your life. A positive thought produces a positive approach, increasing the likelihood of a positive outcome. Keep a positive flow of thoughts and experiences in your life. You will be amazed at how wonderful it feels, and how much it enhances your life on a daily basis. Find the positive in all things and in all situations. Become an optimist!

> *Donna was running late for work, but she needed to stop at the bank to make a deposit. When she got to the bank, only the drive-through lanes were open; the bank was otherwise closed. Donna was concerned at first when there were two cars waiting ahead of her. She was unsure how long they would take and how much later she would be for work. But she chose to think that the process would be quick and easy. She repeatedly thought to herself "quick and easy" until the car in front of her moved up to the window. That car left quickly as its occupant only needed to drop something off at the bank. Donna gladly pulled up to the bank window and made her deposit as planned. She felt grateful that the process was indeed quick and easy.*

Align your thoughts with your intentions. When you feel powerless over circumstances, choose to think positively. Sometimes your only chance to create a positive outcome is to think positively. Choose to think positively regardless of the situation. Positive thoughts produce wonderful—if not amazing—results.

Choose to think that the registration line will be short, that the class will be open, and that the job offer will come. Think that the apartment you want will be available and that the checks you write will go through easily. Think that your roommate will be home on the day that you forget your house keys. Think that the assignment will be easy, and that you will have enough cash with you when you are in the supermarket checkout line. Think that the results will be good, that the bank will approve the loan, and that the sun will shine on your special day.

Think with certainty and not with ambivalence. Thoughtful intentions must be clear and concise. Avoid ambivalence; it causes confusion and creates confusing outcomes. Know what you want to experience, and align your thoughts thusly. Think what you will.

It takes the same amount of effort to be positive as it does to be negative. The difference lies in the outcome. Produce the desired outcome by aligning your thoughts with your intentions.

Think the good, not the bad.
Think ease, not struggle.
Think choice, not sacrifice.
Think happy, not sad.

Are there particular thoughts that you are wrestling with at this time? Are they negative or fearful thoughts? If so, complete the exercise on the next page and transform your negative thoughts into positive thoughts.

> **Think what you want, but think in a way that serves your highest good.**

Finally, believe in yourself. Positive thoughts about situations or experiences are easier when you believe in yourself. You are capable. The classic children's book *The Little Engine That Could* is a reminder to all of us of the power of thoughts. When preparing for a challenge, start by thinking that you can meet it and accomplish it: "I think I can."

Choose to believe that all things are possible, regardless of how they appear to you. As you move through the challenge, your thoughts will change from "I think I can" to "I know I can." As you engage in the experience, you will be able to exercise your belief in yourself. As you complete the challenge, you shift to the acknowledgment of "I can!" Believe in yourself and create a life of abundance.

Your success on the path of abundance is dependent on what you believe. You choose what you believe about yourself, about your life, and about your dreams. Choose to believe that all things are possible, and that even the sky is not the limit. And then sit back and observe how life unfolds before you.

Transforming negative thoughts into positive thoughts.

Write down any negative thoughts that are sabotaging your abundance. Rewrite each negative thought as a positive thought. For example, the negative thought *I am not good enough* can be written as *I am good enough*.

Align your thoughts with what you want to manifest.
Refer to these positive thoughts whenever you're thinking
in an undesirable way. Turn your thoughts to the positive.
Celebrate the desirable outcomes!

Negative Thoughts

_____
_____
_____
_____
_____
_____
_____
_____
_____
_____

Positive Thoughts

_____
_____
_____
_____
_____
_____
_____
_____
_____
_____

CHAPTER SIX

The Art of Visualization

If you can dream it, you can do it.

Walt Disney

Visualization is an art; it requires a creative imagination. But many people are quick to surrender their creative imagination and to embrace realism. They are afraid of feeling disappointed, so they convince themselves that they must "see it to believe it." They have forgotten how to dream.

Because it is a vital form of creative expression, art encourages dreaming; if you can dream it, you can make it. This philosophy is also true with regard to attracting abundance. As is true of art, life is whatever you make it. Artists choose the colors and the medium with which they will creatively bring an object or experience to life. Creativity guides the entire artistic process and artists are willing to make mistakes, which they embrace as a part of the process. Creativity is then enhanced, as artists transform mistakes into works of art.

If only you viewed life in this same way! You would perceive mistakes as opportunities to create something better than you could possibly have imagined before you made the mistakes. Mistakes create opportunities.

Viewing life in this way allows you to see the best in all situations. You will find peace and contentment in life's uncertain circumstances. You can make lemonade out of lemons. You will believe that whatever happens is what is meant to happen.

Life does not consist of mistakes,
only unforeseen opportunities.

Just as an artist takes a colored pencil to paper, so you can bring a positive outlook to the events in your life. You may be unsure of what will happen in your life, but you can choose to trust that it will be good. Life is good—and therefore anything that happens in life, even the unexpected, is potentially good. Many artists possess the ability to visualize their art prior to starting the physical process of drawing, painting, or sculpting. As a result, their visualization guides them through the process of physically creating their works of art.

Are you a visual person? Can you see your dreams and desires in your mind before their physical manifestation? Can you see the future academic degree hanging on your wall? Can you see your house in the country or your own business in your community? Can you see yourself living in a different part of the country? Can you see yourself married or taking care of a child? What are you able to see for yourself and for your life?

What are you willing to imagine?

Although everyone possesses an imagination, few people use their imaginations for their own benefit. Many people can imagine bad things happening, but find it difficult to visualize positive events and results. People also resist their imaginations and choose to stick to the facts. Such people feel secure with facts, not fiction. Facts are necessary and important, but they limit your vision.

The imagination is powerful. It allows us to think in creative and open-ended ways. Anything is possible. Your imagination formulates your dreams. What would happen if you imagined your dreams coming true? More importantly, what *could* happen?

Children are free to dream and to utilize their active imaginations. Adults, on the other hand, are forced to "get serious." As an adult, you are pushed into reality while feeling confused and uncertain about what you want to do with your life. Society determines your needs based on time. You are told that it is time to get a job, time to go to college, and time to get married. Our society believes in the philosophy of "get moving for fear that time will be wasted."

Unfortunately, this philosophy does not always take into consideration your dreams or level of preparedness. You probably feel pressured to make decisions that may affect the remainder of your life. If you decide to get married or move overseas, your life will shift. Time pressures contribute to lost and abandoned dreams.

You might enlist in the military because you don't know what else to do. You only know that it is time to do *something*. When you feel pressured to make a decision, you react. Your decisions are then determined by time pressures and not by your desires.

Although it is time to do *something*, are you certain about what it is that you want to do? Or are you simply reacting to the demands of society and to the pressures of time? Once you leave high school, the pressure is on to dive right into an unfamiliar and scary world. In some ways, this leap into the unknown resembles the birth process. The infant in the womb who is being pushed out into the world by some unknown force has no idea what is happening. Life has a way of pushing you forward, whether you feel ready or not. You feel pressured to make decisions before knowing what you want for your life. The more pressure you feel, the faster you move, with little thought about where you are going or how the pressure will impact you later.

Take the necessary time to develop and understand your direction in life. Head toward your dreams rather than going where the pressure you feel takes you. Make conscious decisions rather than fear-based decisions. People commonly fear that they will miss the boat and lose out on their dreams. However, if you take the time to make deliberate decisions, you will be on the boat regardless of its time of departure. After all, your dreams are your own and *you* determine when and how they sail.

The ability to visualize your dreams enables you to prepare for the good and prevents you from surrendering to fear. Visualization prepares you for your desired future. It gives you the necessary time to identify your dreams prior to their manifestation.

Visualization is based on establishing goals. Goal-setting serves a valuable purpose in creating the life of your dreams. Goals provide the direction of your journey. Where are you going?

January has traditionally been the month to pause and create resolutions and goals for the new year ahead. It is a time to build dreams. Develop goals rather than resolutions.

Resolutions are temporary and are typically surrendered hours or days later. On the other hand, goals allow you to travel the distance required to make a difference in your life. Write your goals down for enhanced visibility. That which is seen tends to manifest more quickly than the unseen. Revisit your goals throughout the year to keep them up to date. You do not want to manifest something that you no longer desire.

Visualization allows you to see your goals and your dreams realized. Through visualization, you can imagine yourself graduating from college or teaching a classroom of children. Visualization enables you to close your eyes and see what your desires look like prior to their physical manifestation. Your dream home comes alive in your mind's eye. You can visualize yourself in a particular career or driving a certain vehicle.

Some people can visualize places, things, and other people with ease. They are able to close their eyes and envision detailed pictures. Other people close their eyes but are not able to see anything. What is the difference? How can some people visualize so easily while others are not able to do so? The answer relates to the differences between people's minds.

Visualization is nothing more than the ability to dream. Some people are natural dreamers. They dream or fantasize without much effort. They stare out windows or daydream while engaged in mundane tasks. It appears to others as if these people aren't doing anything. Yet their minds are actively engaged in creating and orchestrating various details. The minds of dreamers are active, not idle. Dreamers are able to go beyond what is in front of them and explore a wider sphere of knowing. They are gifted with the ability to see beyond reality and to reach into the domain of unlimited possibilities. They are able to go beyond what is happening before them—and envision the possibility of what *could* happen.

Dreamers bring their dreams to life, unbeknownst to onlookers. Although some dreamers are daydreamers, dreamers include an array of people, all of whom entertain the possibility that dreams can come true. Unfortunately, society judges dreamers as inattentive or unavailable, when in fact creativity is at work and their minds are developing ideas to use later. Creative people typically struggle in school because their minds work differently from those of non-creative people. They are expected to think as the majority thinks, when in fact they think differently. Dreamers have a natural ability to visualize, and therefore they possess a vital key to abundance. Every person possesses the ability to dream, but few give themselves full permission to experience their dreams.

Allow yourself to dream.

Aid yourself in the process of visualization by becoming comfortable with *being* instead of doing. Sit awhile. Close your eyes and be with whatever thoughts or feelings emerge. Do not censor the information by picking through the details. When you believe that all things are possible, you can dream without criticism. Criticism deflates the ability to dream. It calculates the dream in terms of reality and it leads you to immediately dismiss your dreams. There is no point in dreaming if you believe that it is impossible for your dreams to come true.

Dreams do not have to fit perfectly with reality; they are simply a starting point from which you can identify what you want in life. Dreams happen automatically when your mind is given the freedom to dream. Dreams are not right or wrong. As is true for nocturnal dreams, daydreams convey information. You may be intrigued by the meaning of dreams. You may be afraid to dream, and think that dreams are silly or meaningless. Regardless of what you believe about dreams, the ability to dream is important. Dreaming is a natural state of the mind. Yet most people substitute busy thoughts for daydreaming opportunities. They prefer to think than to dream.

Give yourself permission to dream.

Thoughts will easily push you off the path to abundance, as thoughts impose a catalog of details that interfere with your specific dreams. Imagine that your dream is to visit Hawaii in the next year. Unfortunately, within minutes of daydreaming about Hawaii, your thoughts take over. You think of all the reasons why it isn't possible to travel to Hawaii: you don't have the money. You won't be able to get the time off from work or school. You have too many commitments. Your parents won't approve.

As a result of all these thoughts, you quickly dismiss your dreams.

Abundance is abundant; it has no limits. Thoughts, on the other hand, are limited. As discussed earlier, thoughts are obstacles on your path to abundance. If you are like most people, you stop dreaming as soon as you come to a thought that opposes your dreams. You surrender. You find yourself unable to see beyond the obstacle, and so you proceed to abandon your dreams. You end up believing that you can't go to Hawaii because of the various details involved.

How many times have you abandoned your dreams and desires with your mere thoughts? It is time to change your thinking! In a life of abundance, it is important to move beyond preconceived obstacles and limitations. If money is often an obstacle on your path, ask yourself the question, "If money weren't an issue, would I go to Hawaii?" Move out of your thoughts and into unlimited possibilities.

Abundance is life without limits. Yet most people limit their dreams and desires. They decide what they can and cannot do based on the facts in front of them. Know that the Universe does not see lack and limitation in the ways that we do. The Universe only knows abundance. Choose to think as the Universe thinks!

Visualization allows you to dream without limitations.

Visualize what could be possible, instead of limiting yourself to what you *think* is possible. What you choose to think is only a droplet when compared to the ocean. Its relevance is insignificant to the greater plan for your life. Always think in terms of your dreams. What do you want to happen? Think big. Then think bigger.

Keep in mind that you are dealing with the Universe, a powerful and mysterious spiritual force. Anything is possible. Although you are unsure about the details of how your dreams will manifest, you must continue to invest in your dreams. Believe that all things are possible. It is not necessary to know *how* things will happen. Just know that they *will* happen: somehow, somewhere, someday.

Believing in your dreams is a prerequisite for abundance. It is all right to leave many of the details to the imagination. Dare to dream! Ask for what you want, and leave the details up to the Universe. There is a great deal that you do not know about life. Relinquish control and allow yourself to be pleasantly surprised. Let go of your tendency to ask *how, what, when,* and *why.* Surrender the details. Your job in dreaming is to simply ask for what you desire. Refer to your Desires Checklist and begin to visualize your dreams in physical form.

What do you want in your life?

Visualization is a powerful tool in the manifestation of dreams. Imagine that you have had a dream, since you were a child, of living in Florida. Can you close your eyes and visualize your life in Florida? Can you see the palm trees? If you are not able to see them, can you feel the energy of being in Florida? Can you feel the warmth of the radiant sunshine?

Visualization uses numerous senses. Can you hear the birds and the ocean? If you want to own a restaurant, can you see yourself engaged in the restaurant business? What are you wearing? What are you doing? What does your daily life look like when you own this type of business?

Visualization is an art. It is a process through which your dreams come to life. There is not a right way or a wrong way to visualize your dreams. In fact, visualization is always right. It simply requires effort. You must make the time to visualize your dreams and desires.

Visualization needs a quiet place. You cannot effectively visualize while you are driving a car or watching television. Visualization requires you to block out the external world in order to gain awareness of your internal world. Your dreams are tucked deep inside you, longing to be expressed. To see and experience your dreams, you must go within. If you are restless, it will take time to simply sit and close your eyes. If you are ambivalent about the process, you may be easily distracted, particularly in the beginning. As is true of most things in life, visualization becomes easier with practice. Get acquainted with the process one step at a time:

1. Sit comfortably.
2. Sit quietly.
3. Close your eyes for a few minutes.
4. Close your eyes for a longer period of time.
5. Breathe.
6. Quiet the mind.
7. Allow visions, sounds, or experiences to develop.

It may take longer to master one step than the others. Your first attempt may create feelings of frustration and impatience.

Be patient with yourself and with the process. After all, you are a beginner. Positive results come from doing it, not from doing it quickly. It may take you a week to be able to sit quietly. Work within your comfort zone, and take your time feeling comfortable at each stage rather than pushing yourself to your desired outcome, the ability to visualize your dreams. Visualization is a process, and successful visualization is based on your ability to sit with the process. What happens is what needs to happen. If you are not able to visualize initially, accept that. That is also part of the process. Be willing to sit with the experience. When you do, amazing things will occur.

Abundance requires patience. In the delivery of your dreams and your desires, you must be patient with yourself, with the process, and with the Universe. As you learn to visualize, you are also learning these other significant components to prosperity and abundance.

Visualization also takes practice; it is a learned skill that requires time and persistence. It is not something that you can just think about doing. You must actually do it. Sit comfortably with your eyes closed and create the opportunity for visualization to occur. Experience makes the process comfortable.

Visualization is fun. Just as it is enjoyable to design a dream home or to plan an ideal wedding, it is also fun to dream about and envision your desires. Wondering about and "trying on" your dreams before they manifest is exciting. Doing so motivates you to move forward on your path to creating a life of fulfillment. Visualization helps you to see that your dreams can come true.

Justin planned to build a house from the time he was ten years old. With each passing year, he added to his catalog of ideas and desires. He knew what he wanted in his house, from the fireplace to the Jacuzzi tub in the master bedroom. He drew a layout on paper, and he stayed true to this dream. It motivated him to pursue a college education and a prosperous career. Justin was determined to make his dream come true.

Visualization becomes easier with time and practice. If, after regular practice, you remain unable to visualize your dreams, you can create an alternate physical visualization of your dreams and desires. Take a poster board and glue words and pictures on it that represent your dreams and desires. If you want to attract a loving relationship, find words that best define such a relationship and include them on your poster. Include pictures of wedding rings to symbolize marriage or a palm tree to represent a vacation to a warm-weather destination. Choose words that complement your pictures.

In the center of the poster board, glue an image or word that represents your spirituality. Cut out the word "God" or a picture of a tree or a cross. Choose whichever image or word correlates to your personal spiritual beliefs. By placing this particular symbol on the poster, you acknowledge the Universe, God, or Higher Power as the source of your abundance. God is the vital force behind the physical manifestation of your dreams.

With magazines and scissors at your side, cut out pictures and words that represent your desires. Include on your poster elements of your ideal life such as marriage or a family, a financially secure job, a home, a vacation, or a college diploma. Your poster is a visual presentation of your dreams and desires, a physical representation of what you want to manifest in your life. Creating a poster is time well spent and fun to do. Keep your poster in a place where you can look at it on a daily basis.

Visualization invites your dreams to come closer. When you visualize your dreams, you communicate to the Universe that you are invested in your dreams. You are demonstrating that you want your dreams to come true, you believe that they will come true, and you are engaging the help of the Universe in making that happen. Visualization prepares the way for your dreams to manifest. You can see your dreams come alive before they actually manifest. Visualization allows you to prepare for this welcome blessing. It pushes your dreams toward manifestation.

Patience is a necessary prerequisite for the manifestation of your dreams. Avoid feeling disappointed or discouraged when your dream does not manifest immediately. Dreams always manifest at the right time, even if it is not on your schedule. Be patient with yourself and with the process. These are your dreams, and they deserve your patience and persistence. Allow your dreams and desires time to develop. Do not be in a hurry, or you will end up settling for less that what you truly desire. Spend time in the dreaming phase. Visualize your dreams as you patiently anticipate their arrival.

Focus your visualization on the manifestation of one dream at a time. Visualization sets your intention. Do not confuse the Universe by visualizing various things at the same time. Identify what you would like to manifest first. Once your dream materializes, you can then move on to the next dream.

Similarly, do not clutter your poster board with too many pictures and words. Leave space open. Maintain a sense of clarity and order in the process of manifesting your desires. If all your dreams materialize at once, or in a sudden manner, you'll be overwhelmed. You may then resent the manifestation of your dreams and react by pushing your dreams back into the invisible plane. Allow your dreams to materialize at their own pace. Don't rush them. Visualize your dreams coming true, one dream at a time and in the order of your priorities.

Right livelihood.

For many people, their most important dream is to find work that is fulfilling and meaningful. Work is the means by which we achieve financial and material abundance. Work is an integral component of the American Dream. Although most people are in hot pursuit of the American Dream or their own culture's equivalent, few succeed in living it. They may become wealthy and acquire material possessions, but they still lack the feelings of gratitude and contentment that lock it all in place. Abundance includes loving life and loving what you do with your life.

Work consumes a great deal of our waking hours. The typical person works forty or more hours each week, not including the time eaten up getting to and from work. Work is how people pay their bills and live their chosen lifestyles. Unless you were born into great wealth, you must support your life through work.

Too often people fall into a certain job or career. In other words, they take what they think they can get. Decisions are typically based on availability and convenience rather than on choice. Perhaps your mother was a nurse who got you a job at the local hospital, where the pay and the benefits are good. If you need the paycheck, it forms the basis of your decision to accept the job.

Maybe you have taken a job in order to earn a paycheck or you have changed jobs for the same reason—to earn a bigger paycheck. You work "for a living," to pay your bills. You probably work to have more in your life: more material possessions such as cars or boats. As a result, you may also resent your job because it is something you have to do in order to pay your bills.

Work is the primary means for achieving abundance. You should therefore choose your work because it fulfills you and because you enjoy it rather than because of the paycheck. Life fulfillment does not come from a paycheck, but from feeling happy and content. Avoid the mistaken belief that if you earn more money, you will automatically be happy. Money rarely brings happiness. Find work that you enjoy—and the money will come.

As you look for your ideal career, keep your desires in mind. Use visualization to assist you in finding work that is right for you. Don't just "take a job" in order to get a paycheck. Although you may need to start somewhere lower on the totem pole than you'd like in order to gain knowledge and experience, recognize your early jobs as temporary situations. They serve as stepping stones on the way to doing what you truly want to do. Choose work that will serve your larger ambitions, and that is in line with your ultimate desires. Move in the direction of your desired career.

Experiment, experience, and enjoy.

Be willing to experiment in different jobs. Experience what it's like to work in different settings and with different kinds of people. Don't allow others to pressure you to decide what you will do for a living and for the rest of your life. Give yourself some needed breathing room. Give yourself time to experiment with your desires and to discover your interests. If you like the idea of being a doctor, work in a medical office or hospital to get an inside perspective. If you discover that you don't like the medical field, choose something else. Despite how others might react, there is no shame in trying something. Follow your dreams.

Avoid associating failure with any particular job. When you impose a feeling of failure on yourself, you block yourself from moving forward on your path to abundance. You put up an obstacle that stands between you and success. You *can't* fail on the beginner's path to abundance, where there are no grades or evaluations but only experiences. Move forward. Don't marry the first job that comes along. Have the courage to experiment and to discover what work you enjoy the most. You will be working for a long time, so find work that really suits you.

Careers tend to imply fixed or permanent positions. Jobs, on the other hand, are often temporary and merely something to do for a while. Throughout your life, you may have numerous jobs but only one or two careers. Consider the jobs that you have had so far in your life. Make a list of these jobs and examine what each of them has taught you. Review this list and identify the skill, strength, or type of knowledge that you have gained from each experience. Add them up and you will discover the components of your right livelihood—the work that is right for you and that you were meant to do on this planet.

> **You have been groomed to discover
> your right livelihood.**

Your early experiences will guide you in the direction of your right livelihood. It is work that comes naturally to you. It is meaningful and fulfilling. Your right livelihood is the culmination of all that you have enjoyed from each of your jobs. It is built on what you love to do—work you enjoy and look forward to doing. It is fun and exciting work that you would choose to do even without a paycheck. Choose work that is right for you. Choose your right livelihood.

> *Janice has had the following jobs since she was a teenager: newspaper delivery person, cashier at a supermarket, and an activity aide at a nursing home. In examining the strengths of these jobs, she discovered that she enjoyed helping people. She noticed that at each of these jobs, she preferred to move at her own pace. She liked the flexibility of being creative and the structure of being organized. She valued the importance of having fun at work, since she is a naturally playful person. These components helped Janice to realize her desire for personal interaction*

with people, her interest in providing a service, and her preference for making things fun for others. She eventually found a career in a childcare setting that she loves. Janice discovered her right livelihood.

How do I find my right livelihood?

Sadly, most people never find their right livelihood. They take a job and may not look for another job for many years, if at all. They settle for the paycheck, and for a job in their comfort zone. They already know how to do their jobs and don't want to learn different skills. Additionally, they are convinced that they cannot successfully do any other job. Or they are convinced that they will never get the same pay or benefits if they go somewhere else.

Don't buy into such beliefs. Right livelihood requires you to keep moving until you find what's right for you. Have the necessary courage to explore different jobs and careers.

It is easier to take a job than it is to move into your right livelihood. Right livelihood requires both courage and patience. It requires risk. It is challenging to wait for the right career to come along. People may pressure you to "just get a job."

Of course, most of us need to work. Sitting idly by and not earning money will rarely allow our dreams to materialize. However, you do not need to treat a job as a lifetime career. Don't settle for less than what you truly want. It is difficult to give up a good paycheck. But when you take a job solely because of pay or benefits, you settle for less than what you desire.

Pay and benefits represent security. Taking a job based on the hope of security reflects a fear of starvation or homelessness. The need for security is a fear that you will not survive. Hence, security is based on a fear of not having what you need. Security is the fear of scarcity. Security represents the illusion of a cushion surrounding your fears of being without or of not having enough. Security is the sacrifice that you make in order to avoid scarcity. If you are afraid of being without, you may end up taking a job that you dislike and staying in it until you retire.

Give up the fear of failing, the fear of succeeding, or the fear that you will not have what you need. We live in a society that reinforces financial and material rewards, and that tells us we have a good job if we make good money and live in a large house. Our society believes that doing what we love must entail sacrifice. However, you sacrifice a great deal more when you settle for a job that is not satisfying and that ultimately strangles your desires.

If you must change jobs every two years prior to discovering your life work, that is fine. Do not let others shame you for moving toward work that is fulfilling. In each job you hold, you learn additional skills and acquire more knowledge. It is all right to move around and to change jobs to improve your life. Don't let thoughts of scarcity or fearful feelings stand in your way of loving life. A paycheck will rarely determine your level of satisfaction and joy in life. Be patient in order to discover your life's work, the kind of work that serves you and that you are meant to do. Choose work in line with your interests and desires.

What would I love to do?

Experience the emotional surge that is derived from visualization. Visualize all that you desire, including your ideal work. Invest in your dreams and do what you can to bring them to fruition. Think, believe, and visualize. Appendix B of this book includes a guided meditation for discovering your life's work. Visualize for fun and visualize to imagine your desired future. With the consistent use of visualization, you will step lively toward the fulfillment of your dreams.

Goals and desires exercise

Instructions: In the chart on the next page, write down your personal and professional goals and desires. List them in order of significance. For example, buying a new home may be a higher priority for you at the present time than going back to college. Therefore, the goal of buying a new home should be numbered higher—i.e., #1—than the latter goal on your priority list. Goals are easier to accomplish when they are broken down into smaller, more concrete steps.

Your Personal Goals and Desires

Priority List	Goals/Desires	Steps Toward Completion	Accomplishment Date

Your Professional Goals and Desires

Priority List	Goals/Desires	Steps Toward Completion	Accomplishment Date

CHAPTER SEVEN

Proclamation: Voicing Your Desires

When your heart is in your dream,
no request is too extreme.

Jiminy Cricket

Most people have been talking since before the age of two. But now it is necessary for you to learn how to talk in a way that will move you down the path of abundance. Understand the way you currently communicate while also discovering the communication methods that will bring your dreams to light. Words are powerful and are the most effective way of manifesting your desires. What are you saying about your desires and your dreams? Watch your words, as your words follow up on your thoughts. If you think negatively, you are at risk for using words that directly oppose your dreams and desires. You will be more likely to communicate what you do *not* want to happen rather than what you do want.

Most people say things in a negative rather than a positive way. They commonly use words such as *can't*, *won't*, and *don't*. They say, "I can't afford to buy a house," "I'll probably never get married," and "I don't have the money."

Are you aware of how you commonly use words and what their impact is on the manifestation of your dreams? Watch your words. Negative phrases will sabotage your desired future, whether that future is later today or during the next several years. Your choice of words will either invite your dreams to come forward or else it will push them away from you. Negative words oppose the attraction of the good in life.

Negative phrases communicate what you don't want to happen: *I won't get that job. I can't afford a new car now.* But the truth is that you *do* want that job. You do want to be able to afford a new car. So why speak aloud negative phrases? Why are you communicating what you *don't* want to happen?

Most people have been conditioned to communicate in this way, to talk negatively about their lives and desires. Words readily communicate their fears. If you are like most people, you choose words that prepare yourself for disappointment, rather than choosing words that communicate what you want to experience. We live in a culture that discourages us from "getting our hopes up." Instead, we are encouraged to prepare for disappointment.

Perhaps you believe that it is more important to prepare for disappointment than to invite your dreams to come closer. You might even think that an experience is more likely to turn out in the way you want it to if you say something that opposes your desires. Superstition still plays a part in many people's lives and in their beliefs about their future.

Disappointment is a common emotion you feel when you expect one thing but receive another. It represents the inability to embrace the unexpected. As you move further along your path, the feeling of disappointment diminishes. It is difficult to feel disappointed amidst a life of true abundance. Drop your current ways of speaking and embrace communication that is conducive to an abundant life.

Distance yourself from all communication that impedes the development and manifestation of your dreams. Avoid the temptation to complain. The tendency to complain will gradually diminish as you move further down the path to abundance. Complaining drains the energy from your desires. Complaints flow as easily and as readily as a river with a strong and consistent current. You can start the day complaining. You can complain that the shower was not hot enough, that your car is making a noise, and that there was too much traffic on the way to work. You can complain about work. You can complain about people. It's easy to drown in complaints because, sadly, you can always choose to complain about something.

Complaining is an ineffective means of communication. Complaining also keeps your desires at bay. After all, what would you have to complain about if your dreams manifested? Complaints represent unhappiness and discontent. Replace complaining with your true desire to feel happy and to live a rich and abundant life. It is a rewarding exchange. Choose to communicate effectively rather than to complain. As the saying goes, "Complaining will get you nowhere." That is also notably true on the path to abundance. Complaining often represents a need for attention. People will like and respect you more for not complaining.

Gossiping about others is another common example of communication that impedes abundance. Gossiping is a form of complaining about another person. The adult form of "tattling" that young children commonly engage in, gossiping includes talking behind someone else's back and involving a third party rather than having the courage to directly discuss a problem with the source of the problem.

Don't gossip! Focus on what *you* are saying or doing, rather than focusing on the actions of other people. If you must focus on what other people are doing, choose to look for what they did right. Notice what the person has done well. Tell others what you've found. Speak praise, rather than spread gossip. Doing so will move you farther along your path to abundance.

Sarcasm and criticism are other common forms of ineffective communication. Sarcasm is a way to get attention within the context of criticism. Sarcasm is humor at the expense of someone else. It is usually used by people who don't feel comfortable conversing with others. The sarcastic communicator is often insecure and is trying to be included or gain acceptance. Most often the use of sarcasm backfires, since people grow tired of sarcastic comments. Such comments become difficult to listen to after a while. The result is that people eventually steer clear of sarcastic and critical communicators.

Unlike the sarcastic person who might be able to elicit a laugh, the critical communicator will drain your energy in minutes. No one wants to be criticized. Critical comments diminish your self-esteem and affect your self-worth. When you are being criticized, you are being blamed for something—including that which is beyond your control. Criticism often brings on feelings of shame: *Shame on you for doing that* or *You should have known better.*

When you feel criticized or shamed, you may either react defensively or shut down emotionally. You try not to hear the critical statements, but the criticism continues to find its way into your unconscious mind. In fact, it is often easier to remember critical comments than it is to recall compliments or praise. Regardless of the experience, criticism hurts, and unfortunately it hurts for a long time.

Swearing is another form of communication that impedes your abundance. If you swear, you are trying to make a point, albeit in a harsh and negative way. Swearing demands attention; it's a way in which people demand power and authority. Swearing often starts out as an attempt to be "cool." It represents a subconscious need to be heard by others.

The use of swear words can be inherited from one's parents. Parents are surprised when their small and innocent child says a swear word, but as is true of many things within our culture, swearing is a behavior often repeated by the next generation. In other words, if your father swore when he felt angry or frustrated, you are also likely to swear when you're feeling frustrated or angry. This behavior, despite being inappropriate or negative, is condoned when others in your family do it too.

Many people don't realize that swearing is a form of emotional abuse. If you swear at someone, you are abusing that person in the same way that name-calling is abusive. Moreover, when you swear *in front of* other people, you are inadvertently abusing those people. Of course, if the person in front of you is also swearing, it will feel like less of an emotional violation.

The use of unkind or hurtful words will sabotage your abundance. When you use words to punish other people, you sabotage the manifestation of your dreams. Words are not meant to be used as ammunition to attack others, but rather as a means to effectively communicate our thoughts and feelings. In addition, the absence of words, commonly referred to as the "silent treatment," will also sabotage dreams.

Ineffective methods of communication will always delay or sabotage your abundance and the good things in life. People who rely on ineffective communication are inadvertently displaying their insecurities on their sleeves. They are attempting to disguise or conceal their inadequacies. Ineffective methods of communication tell us more about the communicator than they do about the person or situation being discussed.

Effective methods of communication, on the other hand, encourage dreams to manifest. Positive expression promotes the manifestation of dreams. Use only words that are positive and that affirm what you want to experience and what you hope to achieve. If you include words that support and encourage your dreams, your chosen words will lead you in the direction of your dreams. Effective communication includes the use of clear and concise phrases that communicate your desires: "I will have a house in the country." "I am on my way to being successful." "I have what it takes to get that promotion."

Unlike ineffective communication, during which you want to avoid the person who is talking, effective communication lures you into sitting awhile and absorbing the positive energy that is emitted. The effective communicator is not only conveying valuable information, but such a person also communicates in a way that inspires others. Every thought and word is expressed in a positive way.

Effective communication is the language of abundance. Watch your words, and select words that are positive and encouraging. Choose words that enthusiastically support your dreams. Say what you mean. Say what you hope for, what you believe in, and what you truly desire: "I will build a house." "I will have a financially rewarding career." Use words that convey what you want to experience and what you wish to manifest in your life. In doing so, you will open the channels to abundance.

Proclaim your desires!

If you want your dreams to come alive, you must always speak about them positively. Proclaim them aloud. Some people are reluctant to tell others about their desires. They fear that their dreams will be sabotaged by others' thoughts and opinions. They think that by withholding their desires, they are protecting their dreams from others' negativity, which may also tap into how they feel about themselves and their abilities.

If you believe in yourself, others will have difficulty stealing your dreams from you. As you develop your personal belief in yourself and in your dreams, the influence of other people's opinions will diminish. It will become easier for you to state your dreams out loud. Allow the Universe to hear your dreams. Be courageous enough to overcome your fear of disappointment or judgment by verbalizing your dreams. Proclaiming your dreams communicates your commitment to their manifestation. You don't simply *hope* that your dreams will manifest. You *know* that they will manifest!

The Universe is a "Yes!" Universe.

The Universe always responds with a "yes," particularly to what is said out loud. For instance, if you say, "I will get the promotion," the Universe responds with a "yes" and begins the process of manifestation. However, if you say, "I won't get the promotion," the Universe also responds with a "yes."

The Universe follows your lead by following your spoken words. If you say that you will get a new car by the end of the year, the Universe says "yes." If you say that you won't be able to afford a car by the end of the year, the Universe still says "yes"! The Universe does not distinguish between requests. It simply responds to them. It is therefore always important to speak words that clearly communicate your desires. Avoid ambivalence.

What are you saying?
Is it what you really want to have happen?
Is it what you want to experience?
Is it what you hope to attract to your life?

Choose your words wisely. Say what you mean. The Universe is eager to fulfill your dreams. Speak in terms of what you want to experience and have happen in your life. In this way, the Universe can start the movement toward manifestation. Don't confuse the Universe. Don't say one thing but mean another. Say what you mean. Most people speak randomly and without consideration for the possible impact of their words.

Speak with clarity and purpose. Words are spoken intentions. Know what you are saying at all times. Your chosen words serve either to move your dreams toward you or to push your dreams away. If you notice yourself speaking words that sabotage your desires, you can change the flow of energy by exclaiming, "Cancel! Cancel! Clear!" Proceed to proclaim what you desire.

Words are powerful. Not only do you need to say what you mean, but you must also mean what you say. If you say that you are going to do something, you are more likely to do it. That is an unspoken law of nature.

The truth is that we are more afraid of the judgments of others for not doing what we said we would than we are afraid of any consequences from carrying forth our stated intentions. We are concerned that others will think that we lied or, even worse yet, that we failed. As a result, we are careful about what we say and we are selective about with whom we talk.

People are afraid that their desires will not manifest if they tell others about them. No one wants to feel ashamed if they have to admit later that their dreams didn't come true. Move forward on your path to abundance by investing in your dreams. Say what you mean, and mean what you say. In other words, follow your dreams no matter where they take you.

Words have an impact on your life and on your dreams. Words sit for a while in the corner of your heart, where you can revisit them time and time again. We remember words, particularly when the words are hurtful or shameful. Be mindful of your words and the purposes that you want them to serve. Allow words to help you, instead of letting them hinder you as you travel along life's path.

Speak with kindness and thoughtfulness. Speak with wisdom and knowledge. Speak from the heart and not from the head. Speak words that clearly communicate your desires. Speak with authority and in a way that allows the Universe to know you are invested in your dreams. Speak in a way that communicates that you are worthy of your dreams. Your dreams are out there and the Universe is listening.

Watch your words!

CHAPTER EIGHT

Trust: Bringing Your Desires Closer

God is my strength and power:
and He maketh my way perfect.

II Samuel 22:33

Trust represents an open but unspoken invitation for your desires to come closer. Trust gives your dreams permission to manifest themselves in the way that you have asked for them to manifest. Trust gives you permission to proceed in the direction of your dreams.

Trust is a difficult emotion to truly feel. You can easily say that you are a trusting person, but are you really? Trust is more than just a feeling. It is a particular way that you respond to situations and to circumstances. Just as sadness may be demonstrated through tears, trust exists when you sit back and see what unfolds. Trust is the opposite of fear.

Fear is the automatic response to most situations and experiences in life. Imagine that your refrigerator has broken down and that you have reacted with fear that the repairs will be costly. Your fear then increases as you imagine that the refrigerator repair will only be the start of something worse. Other household appliances might break down as well! As is true for most people, your negative thoughts start taking over and igniting your fear. Fear is the automatic reaction to a situation that you were unprepared for or did not see coming. Fearful people are afraid of the unknown and the unfamiliar.

Fear is a feeling that most people know very well, but choose to keep concealed. After all, it is not socially acceptable to feel afraid. Society views fear as a weakness that must be avoided. Fear is associated with losing control: if you don't know what will happen next, you may react fearfully. But the truth is that no one truly knows what will happen next in life. They simply think that they do.

Life is full of unexpected surprises.

You could win the lottery tonight and your life would take a different course. Likewise, you could break your leg and tomorrow would be completely different from what you imagined. Life is full of unexpected surprises. Is it necessary to feel afraid all the time? Fear has too much power. It has taken down entire nations.

Yet fear is a normal feeling, much like any other. It is important to understand your fears so that you can move beyond them. Fear does not go away simply because you ignore it.

Fear is the primary culprit responsible for your issues related to life and abundance. Fear produces struggle and hardship; it stifles you and prevents you from moving forward. Fear prevents your desires from manifesting into physical form. Fear, unpleasant to feel and experience, will put the brakes on your life of abundance.

Imagine that you are driving along life's highway when you suddenly hit the brakes. Your fear tells the Universe, the source of your abundance, to stop. Fear immediately stops the process of manifesting abundance. The Universe doesn't want to bring you something that you fear; the Universe wants to bring you what you want. Consequently, fear negatively affects the arrival of your dreams and your desired abundance. Fear typically resides at a subconscious level, and often you aren't even aware of what you fear until it surfaces. Examine your fearful feelings.

What am I afraid of?

Fear stands in front of you like a big bully, intimidating you and preventing you from moving forward. And so you don't move forward. You stay where you are and blame the obstacle in front of you: *I can't move to Florida because my brother will be angry if I do*. You believe that your brother's feelings (obstacle) are preventing you from moving to Florida when in fact it is your own fear that is doing so. Fear underlies your consideration of your brother's feelings. In other words, you doubt yourself and your decision, and you're influenced by someone else's thoughts and emotions.

Fear holds you back. Stop blaming the obstacle and identify your fear regarding your dreams. If you want to go to college, what are you afraid of? Are you afraid that you can't do it? Are you afraid that you will fail? Are you afraid that you won't be able to complete a degree or find a job in your field?

Fear contaminates your thoughts and subsequently sabotages your dreams. Fear wants to know what is going to happen before it happens. Anticipatory fear is the fear that precedes a negative experience. When you are afraid that something bad will happen, you prepare emotionally for the worst outcome. Of course, you don't actually know what will happen, but you are preparing yourself for the worst. You then feel relieved when you realize that the situation didn't turn out nearly as badly as you had originally—fearfully—imagined that it would. Anticipatory fear, like every other type of fear, damages your ability to attract abundance. It drains you of your emotional energy well before anything has had a chance to happen. Move beyond your fears and embrace trust. Trust will bring your dreams to fruition.

Trust is the opposite of fear. We can trust when we are not sure what else to do. Trust can feel like we're surrendering: *I surrender. I don't know what else to do.*

Trust becomes the logical default. Trust *is* surrendering, but without giving up. Trust is a prayerful intention during which you hand over a burden or situation to God or to the Universe. Trust enables you to observe and to respond rather than to merely react. You respond with trust or you react from fear. Fear is uncomfortable, and you want to quickly alleviate the discomfort. If you're like most people, you react in order to gain control over an otherwise powerless situation. You yell at someone at the college financial aid office when you're afraid of being denied financial aid, or you say hurtful things to your spouse or partner as she leaves for a weekend away with friends.

Trust looks and acts differently from fear. Trust is passive; it isn't shameful or accusatory. Trust enables you to let things be, and to let go sooner. Situations and circumstances roll off your back more easily. You don't fixate on a hurtful comment for days, weeks, or years. Trust forgives easily. Trust moves forward easily. Trust *encourages*, while fear *discourages*. Trust builds relationships, while fear destroys relationships. Trust builds abundance, while fear inhibits abundance.

Trust is a passive response. Trust gives the illusion of doing nothing when you're actually doing something: you're choosing to trust. Trust is sitting back and waiting to see what will happen. Trust goes one step beyond relaxation. Trust believes even without seeing physical evidence. It believes that something good is going to happen before something good actually does happen.

Trust knows that surprises are good; it knows that whatever you need and whatever is best for you will happen. Trust believes, without seeing. Trust teaches you to "let things happen" rather than to "make things happen." At times, you need to do nothing but simply trust. For these reasons, trust can be difficult to achieve. You often feel pressure to do something—anything—when you experience powerlessness or fear. Trust teaches you the importance of letting go of the outcome or result. Trust allows you to release expectations, and to embrace each experience for what it is and for what it offers.

Learn to trust that whatever is happening or expected to happen will be good. Trust is the awareness that what happens is exactly what is meant to happen. Trust also means anticipating the good rather than the bad. It is a core belief, in the absence of knowledge, that all is well. You don't know what's going to happen. Yet you simply trust that all is well. You can choose to trust that a situation or experience will turn out okay, that things will work out. Trust calls to you on a daily basis through the varied experiences of life—such as an exam, a medical appointment, a relationship, or a work situation. These experiences represent opportunities for you to react with fear or to respond with trust. You will always have opportunities to develop your trust in people, in life situations, and in yourself. Choose to trust rather than to fear.

Trust seems so simple, but it is often difficult to fully accomplish. It is easier to trust if you think you know what is going to happen. But knowing what will happen is not the same as trust. It is fear disguising itself as trust. It is also human nature. Humans are fearful beings. But by choosing to trust, you can feel comfortable despite not knowing what will happen next.

Fear → Reaction
Trust → Response

A fear reaction is sudden and automatic. A trust response is patient and thoughtful. Trust permits events and experiences to evolve and develop, while fear quickly applies the brakes.

Trust has its basis in spirituality.

Trust is a spiritual experience as much as it is a physical and emotional one. People who have a defined spirituality and a belief in a higher power are able to trust more readily than those who lack spirituality. Spirituality provides people with the foundation to trust.

That doesn't mean that those without a defined spirituality can't experience abundance. They just experience it in a different way. Their path is different and often more challenging. They rely heavily on physically creating their abundance. They work long hours, often at the expense of time with family and friends. Such people will sometimes need to miss family dinners and concerts in order to earn money. They may buy lottery tickets, hoping to generate a lifestyle in which they won't have to work as hard. Their pursuit of money and prestige imposes on family time. For these reasons, many people without a defined spirituality choose not to ask for a life of abundance. They associate abundance with sacrifice. They do not want to abandon their families in order to have a nicer lifestyle. They want both time *and* money, and they look for alternative ways of making money so that they can have more time.

Abundance is easier to accomplish through spirituality, which plays a significant part in the manifestation of abundance. Spirituality is the foundation of trust within abundance. Abundance is your gift from the Universe. It is not earned through struggle! It is earned simply by being alive and by being connected to the spiritual source of abundance. Abundance is your spiritual birthright.

Trust invites abundance.

People who trust in a spiritual presence are further ahead in the quest for abundance because they utilize trust in their everyday life experiences. Trust is the knowledge that you are in good hands. If you can trust that you are being cared for by something greater than a physical being, you will be able to move forward with ease. Spirituality allows you to experience life from the perspective of being cared for. You believe that you are being lovingly guided through life.

Spirituality provides comfort and reassurance that no one person can fully provide. Spirituality fills you up with something indescribable but complete. Without spirituality, people often feel lost or empty, as if something is missing from their lives.

In an effort to fill up the emptiness that dwells within, such people often seek comfort in material possessions, job promotions, and relationships. They are on a perpetual journey for more: more money, more accomplishments, and more material possessions. When they acquire or achieve something, they immediately look for something else to acquire or achieve. They appear restless, perhaps changing jobs or relationships only to find that they still feel discontented. Such people rarely feel satisfied. They desperately look to fill themselves up with something from the outside in order to make up for what they're lacking on the inside. As a beginner to abundance, you can avoid this common path.

Spirituality fills the voids within. Spirituality fills us in ways that physical possessions never will. You don't need more possessions; you need a spiritual connection. People who have a spiritual relationship and who possess little in a material sense feel content and satisfied. Likewise, those who have physical wealth and abundance without a defined spiritual relationship often feel discontented and dissatisfied. Despite achieving financial success, they feel as if something is missing. A spiritual connection fills you physically, emotionally, and spiritually. Spirituality enables you to feel fulfilled!

Many people are raised with spirituality in their families of origin. Their families not only gave them a last name, but also a spiritual understanding of life. Such people were raised with the knowledge that life is more than the physical, more than that which can be seen or touched.

Spirituality goes beyond physical limitations, under which you believe that *some* things are possible. Spirituality is the awareness that life exists on a grander scheme. Spirituality provides a larger and broader view of a situation, as exemplified earlier in this book by the story of the mouse in the maze.

With spirituality, we see more. We can see and experience life through greater vision and understanding. Spirituality recognizes that there is a spiritual force behind all that we desire and all that we hope to achieve. Spirituality lights our path. It minimizes the struggle and makes our lives easier.

Spirituality will help you to achieve abundance without the usual sweat and tears. Make room in your life for a spiritual and guiding presence, regardless of what that might look like to you. Research and explore various spiritual beliefs, and identify those specific beliefs that feel most comfortable to you. Find out what nourishes your soul. It doesn't matter what you believe, as long as you do believe. Spirituality teaches you how to trust, and trust invites your desires to manifest physically.

It is okay to begin the process of abundance and to move along the path discovering more about yourself, your beliefs, and your life. Spirituality is a part of that journey. Trust that your journey will guide you to a greater understanding of personal spirituality. Spirituality feels right only when you are ready to experience it.

Spirituality works best when you cultivate it gradually as opposed to when you feel forced to believe in something that you don't really believe. Forced spirituality creates resistance, and people who feel forced to practice spirituality often rebel against it. They associate spirituality with something unpleasant rather than with something pleasant. Anything that feels unpleasant is not likely to be repeated. Allow the time and space for your spirituality to gradually materialize in a pleasant and enjoyable way. Be patient. Attend activities and experiences that cultivate spiritual awareness. Repeat those that feel comfortable and pleasant.

Spirituality is complemented by a network of supportive people. People represent the physical components to any spiritual connection. Therefore, the people you meet in a religious context play a significant part in creating the spiritual atmosphere. "Religious people" are frequently perceived as judgmental and critical of others, a perception that creates walls between those who practice a particular religion and those who do not.

The fear of judgment is a primary reason why people don't develop or adhere to a spiritual practice. Judgment is fear. Judgment closes doors, particularly in environments that preach love and acceptance. Look for spiritual communities that welcome you and that accept you unconditionally.

Trust is the most rewarding way to approach life. It allows you to feel calm and relaxed no matter what else is happening. Trust invites you to accept things as they are, and to accept people and situations for what they are. Life just is. Allow life to unfold in front of you without preconceived notions or expectations. Trust that what is supposed to happen is what indeed will happen.

Trust requires you to wait. Force yourself to sit on your hands and wait. Most people want to avoid the uncomfortable feeling of waiting, and they equate waiting with the fear that they won't have what they need. They want to continuously make things happen in order to avoid having to wait.

It is difficult to wait. If things are visible and moving, then at least it feels as if something is happening. Yet abundance develops in the invisible sphere. You can't see it occurring. For this reason, abundance requires you to wait and to trust.

The need to wait is one reason why people stray from the path to abundance. Such people are not willing to wait; they become impatient and get tired of waiting. They use credit cards to purchase items that they don't have the money to pay for. They want it all *now*, and think they'll pay for it all later.

Our society is built on the premise that people's desires can be satisfied quickly. We've lost our ability to be patient and wait for things. We purchase gas at the pump so we won't need to wait in line. We book vacations online in order to avoid waiting for someone else to confirm availability. We do everything as quickly and as easily as possible. And anytime that we are forced to wait, we feel restless and frustrated.

Waiting is essential for manifesting your dreams.

Trust that your dreams are in the making. Abundance begins in the invisible, and spends a majority of time in the invisible. It is there that your dreams are forming and developing, as if they were a baby growing within its mother's womb. Your dreams have their own birthing process. When they physically manifest, you have completed the process. Trust that your dreams are moving forward through the invisible and anticipate their eventual arrival. Become comfortable with not seeing. It does not mean that your dreams aren't manifesting; it simply means that they have yet to break the surface. Be patient. The ability to wait is the ability to trust. To trust as you wait is a necessary part of manifesting your dreams.

We have multiple opportunities to trust on any given day. Develop your ability to trust in the small experiences of everyday life. Don't wait for big things to happen in order to exercise your trust. Trust that you will arrive on time. Trust that there are enough stamps to mail the important letter. Trust that the bank is open. Trust that you are in good hands and that all is well. Trust that your needs will be met.

Trust in life. Trust that everything in life happens for a reason. Know that your life is being guided. Be patient as your dreams move from the invisible into the visible. Your dreams are on their way. Proceed full speed ahead on your path to abundance.

CHAPTER NINE

Generosity and Abundance: The Relationship between Giving and Receiving

One man gives freely, yet grows all the richer;
another withholds what he should give,
and only suffers want.

Proverbs 11:24

Good people are generous people. Generous people are good people. Each of us strives to be a good person, however we define "good." We perceive ourselves and other people as "good" based on various criteria.

Generosity is highly valued in our culture. Generosity implies that one has a big heart, and is caring and considerate of others. Most generous people give generously in order to help others. Generous people are kind. They give from the heart as well as from the wallet.

What are your judgments about people who are generous? Maybe you assume that generous people have a lot of money, and that they're people who have money to give away. Perhaps you tell yourself that you would give away money too if only you had the money to do so.

These types of judgments are common judgments of others. People judge others from their own insecure feelings. You may judge generous people as having resources that you do not. If that's the case, you might entertain the idea that if you won the lottery, you would give generously to people and to organizations. We all want to be generous givers. More importantly, we want to have the money to give. Most of us wish that we had enough money to give generously in order to benefit someone else. We want to give in a way that will make a difference.

Giving is not determined by your net worth.

You may judge generosity as the ability to give without struggle or hardship. Perhaps you believe that generous people have money that is simply sitting around waiting to be spent on something. You may believe that rich people are able to give generously because they have the resources to do so, and that it won't hurt them to give money away since they have it to give. You might even think that such people *should* give away their money.

We live in a society that strongly believes that you must have in order to give, that the ability to give precedes the ability to be generous. Our society tells us that we must first give before we can entertain the idea of being a generous giver.

Think about what you already give to others. You give your time—helping out with, for example, a community bake sale. You might offer colleagues suggestions for how advertising flyers could attract more business. Or you offer your ideas about the set-up in the local library. You give words of encouragement and support to friends and family. You give gifts on certain holidays.

Why do you choose to give?

Do you give to others as an expression of love or appreciation? Do you give in an effort to show others that you love and care about them? Although these are good reasons for giving, they aren't the most common reasons why people give. Although we all want to give for the right reasons, people often give for the wrong reasons. We want to give unconditionally, without expectations or reason. Yet it is more common to give conditionally, with expectations and reasons.

Sometimes, people give for reasons that are conscious. Such people might give because it makes them feel good. However, there are other reasons for giving as well.

People also give because they feel obligated to do so. They give because it is a specific time noted for giving, such as a holiday or a birthday. They give because they *have* to give. There are times when others expect you to give, and you no doubt have given to others even when you don't necessarily want to.

Even if you don't have the financial means to give, you may give anyway. Perhaps you give because you are afraid of what others will think if you don't. You can give to make others feel better. You give get-well cards and sentiments to cheer up those who are sick or having a difficult time. You give flowers on anniversaries and on other special occasions. Maybe you give to various charities and organizations to support their efforts and services. And you also give when others give to you.

Perhaps you are a person who gives when you feel guilty or ashamed. If that is the case, you may give in an effort to feel worthy and deserving. Maybe you give when you don't know what else to do for someone else, or you may give to feel valued and appreciated. You give to console and to comfort.

You may also give for unconscious reasons. Perhaps you give in an effort to feel better about yourself. Moreover, you may give to others in an effort to be liked. Everyone wants to be liked, and perhaps you buy others something or perform favors for them. You might invest your time, your money, and your energy in order to be liked by others.

Conditional giving is the most common type of giving. It is often accompanied by a feeling of obligation. Conditional giving implies giving because you have to, even if you've convinced yourself that you want to give or that it's the right thing to do:

I give because I have to give.
Aunt Bertha sent me a card on my birthday.
She will be angry if I don't send her a card on her *birthday.*

Conditional giving is often associated with a lack of self-esteem. Conditional givers feel obligated to someone else because of their uneasiness with themselves. They give to others in order to avoid feeling badly about themselves, in an effort to feel better. They don't want to feel guilty or ashamed if they don't give to others, and they fear being judged as selfish or "cheap." Conditional giving is a method for avoiding self-directed negative feelings. It often backfires.

Conditional giving results in feelings of resentment. You eventually resent the obligation to give to others. You start to feel as if you're giving to others all the time, as if you rarely get a fair return when you do so. You wonder when others will give back to you in a similar way. You build walls of resentment that force you to give reluctantly or not to give at all. Yet giving is an integral part of life, and of abundance.

Consider how you feel when you have to pay your monthly bills. Most people resent paying their bills, resent giving their money to other people. They feel denied of their money and of the other things they desire. They associate paying bills with being denied their needs.

Consider this: when you pay bills, it means you are purchasing desired goods and services. Your bills are physical evidence of what you have, not what you're denied. Bills are associated with various items you want, including a home, a car, and an education. In addition, you pay bills in order to heat and light your home. The reality of having such things in your life is a good thing, not a bad thing. Thus, paying for such items is a good thing and not a bad thing, which many people mistakenly perceive it to be.

Bills are a necessary part of living.

Avoid playing tug-of-war with your money or your monthly bills. Bills represent payment for what you have acquired in your life. You can choose to have a few bills or numerous bills, but you will always have bills.

You resent your bills when you are afraid of not having enough. This common fear forces you to hold on to your money, to be frugal and tight-fisted. You end up not wanting to let go of your money for fear that, if you do, you won't have enough.

Fear compels people to hoard money. You may be afraid to give to others because you believe that there is only a limited amount of money to go around. Consequently, when you spend your money, you fear that you won't have any more left. Notice how fear intrudes upon your abundance. Although hoarding will allow you to have money later, it robs you of the experience of living life to the fullest.

Instead, you are forced to live a life in fear, afraid of not having enough money. You become afraid of losing money, afraid that others will take your money away.

Truthfully, most people give away their money without conscious awareness. Such people are uncomfortable having or managing money. They are quick to give it away, but then they wonder why they don't have any money in their wallets; it's as if they have holes in their pockets! They have difficulty holding on to money for any period of time. If they have money, they spend it quickly. It's easy to lose track of money when you're not consciously aware that you're spending it.

Mike thought that he had thirty dollars, but now he can only find fifteen. Where did the other fifteen dollars go? If that sounds like you, know that you certainly aren't alone. Many people feel as if they lose or misplace money, when in fact they are spending it unconsciously. You might go into a local store and spend twenty-five dollars on various items you didn't plan on purchasing. You end up leaving the store trying to figure out what you purchased for twenty-five dollars. After all, you had only intended to purchase a bottle of shampoo for three dollars and fifty-nine cents. What happened? Where did your money go?

Impulsive shopping is a common means by which people give away their money. It can feel like a thrill-seeking adventure to go into a store and discover items on sale. You act as though you may never see those items ever again, and you convince yourself that you must buy them now. It doesn't matter whether or not you need the item right then;

you want to buy it *now*. You think that eventually you'll need the item, and so you should stock up now in order to have it on hand later. Buying something *now* is impulsive shopping: spending money that you didn't plan to spend on something that you don't currently need. Credit cards provide an easy way to shop impulsively. You don't need to have cash with you. You simply use your credit card.

Spending is a form of giving in which you give your money in exchange for a specific item. When you spend money unconsciously, you no doubt perceive it as being taken rather than being given. But you give when you spend your money. Be aware of conscious giving and unconscious spending. Unconscious spending is another fear-based reaction. You spend unconsciously when you're afraid of not having something when you need it—so you justify your desire to buy it now.

As you release fear, you will give unconditionally rather than conditionally. There will no longer be a hidden— unconscious—agenda behind your giving. Unconditional giving means giving without strings attached and without any expectation for receiving something in return. It implies giving with pure love and a desire to give. You simply give because you want to do so. You choose to give from the heart. You give because you feel grateful and satisfied with what you have, and you are delighted to share your good with others.

Unconditional giving attracts abundance.

Abundance is a spiritual energy that moves in a circular pattern. What we experience now, we may remember experiencing before and are likely to experience again. And so it is with abundance. Most of us have had times of abundance in our lives and times of lack and scarcity. Prosperity can fade in and out of a person's life.

Life consists of periods of overflowing abundance and periods of scarcity. The truth is that both of these ways of living are perceptions. You can have ten dollars in your pocket and feel either rich or poor, depending on your perception and feelings. It is the same ten dollars. Yet your perception of those ten dollars changes, based on circumstances and emotions. Ten dollars is a fixed amount. The amount of money doesn't change—only your *perception* of that money changes. Perception is nothing more than how you judge a situation based on your previous experiences and emotions. Perceptions are fear-based. Your perceptions are based on the presence or absence of fear. Thus, you may perceive the ten dollars as either *barely enough* or as *plenty*.

Life is largely built on perception, which is based on experiences of the past, circling around us in other forms. Life is circular, which is easily demonstrated by the seasons of the year. Winter turns to spring, spring turns to summer, summer turns to autumn, and autumn turns again to winter. The maple tree is bare during the winter, but comes alive again in the spring. By summer, the tree provides shelter and shade with its multitude of branches and leaves. In the autumn, its leaves drop to the ground to prepare for the winter.

And so it is in life. There are times of newness and beginnings, and times of endings and death. The moon also moves through phases of newness to completion, only to begin the process over again. Most of life progresses from a start to a completion and back to a start again. Abundance replenishes in the same way that buds on a tree return each spring.

You know at a core level that life is circular. Yet there may be times when you doubt that fact. Fear can take over and convince you that life is linear, with a defined beginning and a permanent ending. Remember that life is circular. Things have a tendency to come back around.

Elements in life, including finances, come back around.

Giving is also circular. Certain holidays are times when we give to others who give to us, when we do a favor for people who were kind enough to have done us a favor in the past.

Giving and receiving have gone together for a long time. Perhaps that is the reason humans were given two hands: one to give with and one to receive with. Yet some people are more comfortable giving than receiving. They want to give to others, but they don't want others to give to them. They feel embarrassed or ashamed when others give them something, especially if they don't have anything to give back in return. They make excuses if someone compliments their appearance. They ask others not to give them gifts or money. They say things such as, "You shouldn't have" or "I wish you wouldn't do that." They resist receiving.

The familiar feelings of shame and unworthiness affect our ability to manifest abundance. We can feel inadequate and therefore unworthy to receive. Appendix A of this book provides an opportunity for you to explore your feelings of unworthiness.

If you feel unworthy, you prematurely rob yourself of the nicer things in life. To enhance your worthiness, learn to receive without resistance. Receive with gratitude instead of with discomfort and shame. Learn to appreciate yourself in the ways that others appreciate you, which they demonstrate when they give to you. You deserve to receive! Simply receive and say thank you. Abundance is your birthright. You deserve all that is good in life. Step forward and receive your good!

Giving and receiving are equally important on the path to abundance. Create balance in your ability to give and to receive. Give without resentment and receive without resistance. Resistance will block the manifestation of your dreams when they try to surface. As a result, it may look as if your abundance is breaking through, only to be delayed for an indefinite period of time. If it feels as if your desires are stuck, improve your ability to give and to receive, thus allowing abundance into your life with a clear path.

Abundance means that there will always be more than enough, requiring you to perceive things from an unlimited perspective. Abandon your limited thinking of "not enough" and adopt such beliefs as "It is enough" and "I have plenty." In truth, you do always have enough. You just don't always think that you do. Know and appreciate when you have enough.

Money given freely and with gratitude is more likely to return.

Money held captive and given reluctantly is less likely to come back to you. Money was intended to be given freely;

it's part of the free spirit that surrounds all of life. When you choose to give money, give it freely and unconditionally. Be thankful for the service or item represented by each of your bills. Say "Thank you for my home" as you write the check for your mortgage. Give thanks for your car payment. Let money leave your hands with love and gratitude.

Give in a way that invites abundance.

Give freely. Imagine if your money were whisked away by a sudden wind. How would you feel? Would you feel afraid and therefore react with panic, chasing after your money? Or would you chuckle and say, "Wow! I can't believe this is happening!" Is your money repelling you or are you letting money go freely? Would you scream for help from others? Would you feel embarrassed that your money is flying away? Would you feel powerless and give up on the situation, reconciling with the financial loss?

That is an extreme example of giving money freely. However, it is important to realize that money passes through our lives as if it were being whisked away. One minute we have money and the next minute we don't. We've given it away. Although people give money away, they are less likely to give money freely. Giving money freely is accompanied by gratitude, not fear. Giving money freely means that we appreciate the opportunity to give.

Give honestly. Give what is right. If you are expected to pay for something, pay for it. Leave an appropriate tip for the wait staff. Pay people back when you borrow money. After all, you borrowed the money in good faith at a time when you needed it. Someone was kind enough to lend you the money. Pay the money back with the same love and gratitude you felt when you borrowed it.

Be an honest giver. Don't argue about money. Don't barter or haggle. Choose to buy or not to buy, but don't expect others to drop their prices. Pay for things honestly. If you owe money to a creditor or lender, be responsible and make payments. If you're struggling, inform them that you'll make a payment as soon as possible.

Be responsible. Don't stick your head in the sand hoping that your debts will somehow disappear. You created the debt, so you must pay for it honestly. Give honestly, whether it is a small monetary amount such as the admission to a talent show, or a large sum such as a car loan.

Payments are a form of giving. Your employer pays you a salary in exchange for your work. How would you feel if you were asked to wait for your paycheck? Yet when you delay payments to your creditors, you are asking them to wait to be paid. Delayed payments create a delay in your abundance. Don't delay or shortchange others. In cheating others, you cheat the Universe. In giving to others, you give to the Universe.

Make payments with love and gratitude. Be thankful for the service or product that you're paying for. Pay your debts lovingly. Send payments with gratitude and multiply your returns. Abundance is based on supply and demand. When you give from the well of abundance, what you have given is easily and quickly resupplied. The more you give, the more you'll have. What you give to others with love is multiplied back to you.

Love multiplies your good.

The Universe is the source of your abundance. Therefore, you don't own money. Money is a gift from the Universe, given to you to use in exchange for goods and services on this earth. You may exchange work for money, but it remains an exchange of energy. You do something and get something in return. Energy is not meant to be held stagnant for long. Energy passes through. Money and other gifts of the Universe are forms of energy passing through your hands. Money is intended to be given freely.

When you give, you are inviting the Universe to give to you in more abundant ways. You may not know specifically how the Universe will give to you or in what monetary denomination, but you can trust that the Universe will take care of you.

For instance, imagine that you need four hundred dollars for books for college courses. You feel frustrated that you have yet to manifest the money. However, you have had a classified ad in the paper for a roommate for several weeks. While you are worrying about the money for your books, you get a response to the ad and welcome the additional financial benefit of having a roommate. You realize that you will save two hundred dollars for the next eight months. The Universe has sent you the money in a surprising but alternative way. You now have sixteen hundred dollars instead of four hundred.

The Universe may not always deliver your good in the way you expect it. Sometimes, you ask for a present in a green box with a gold ribbon, but the Universe delivers something different. Be careful. You might easily dismiss your good if you are not open to receiving your good in all ways. Perhaps the Universe is delivering you a red box with a white ribbon. Will you recognize it as your good?

Tithing and abundance

Tithing is an ancient form of giving that is described throughout the Bible. A tithe is defined in *Webster's Deluxe Unabridged Dictionary* as "a tenth of the annual produce of one's land . . . or its equivalent for the support of the church or the clergy." In other words, tithing means giving ten percent of one's income to the church or spiritual organization where one receives spiritual nourishment. Tithing is spiritual giving, an offering of a specific monetary amount to a church or synagogue as a means of supporting one's spiritual life.

Churches and other places of worship cost money to maintain and operate. Yet ministers and priests earn little if anything to support themselves, not to mention to pay operating expenses. They rely on donations and other funds to keep the lights on and to provide the community with a place to worship.

Tithing allows churches and synagogues to function financially. Yet only a few religions actually require tithing. For instance, Catholics are encouraged to give, but they are not required to tithe. Thus, many Catholics give minimally to their church. Such people may have observed their parents and grandparents throwing random change or a single dollar bill into the weekly collection basket. As a result, some of them still give only a dollar despite the actual costs of running a church.

Other people are generous givers. They give generously to their chosen church or spiritual organization. They donate money for certain items used by the church or for improvement purposes.

> *Give generously and the Universe will reward you*
> *in unimaginable ways.*

Tithing is giving back to the Universe with gratitude. It demonstrates that you are grateful for all that you have and all that you have been given. Tithing recognizes that the Universe has blessed you, and continues to bless you, physically, financially, and materially.

Many people feel uncomfortable tithing. They perceive tithing as an obligation to give money. They feel forced to give their money to a church or synagogue. They perceive places of worship as "free," and therefore they don't want to give them money.

Such people often make excuses for why they don't tithe. They argue that they don't have the money to give, or that the place of worship doesn't need the money. Some people believe that the funds will be used inappropriately. They may question some of the beliefs and decisions of their religion and its leaders, and therefore they don't want their money to serve as a reward for that with which they disagree. For these people, tithing is conditional giving.

Yet the Bible describes tithing as unconditional giving. Those who tithe are meant to give because they want to support and maintain their preferred place of worship.

Practice the 2 Gs of abundance:
giving and gratitude.

The relationship between organized religion and spirituality has weakened. In the past, church attendance was an integral part of life. Society valued Sunday as a day of worship and family togetherness. For Christians, Sunday was considered a day of rest from the other six days of the week. Stores and other businesses were closed, which allowed people to attend church as a family and to share in the fellowship of their communities. People cooked special meals, spent valuable time together, and visited extended family members such as grandparents or cousins.

For a great number of people, Sundays are no longer a day of rest and spiritual worship. Sunday is now the day often set aside for getting "caught up," for running the errands that there wasn't time for during the rest of the week. Christians may or may not take the time to go to church.

Church attendance now competes with various Sunday-morning activities, such as sporting events, music lessons, and household errands. There are many other places that people would rather be than in church, and church attendance and tithing have decreased over the past few decades. People's resistance to tithing generally increases when they're not attending a particular church or synagogue. They don't want to pay for something that they're not using regularly.

Spirituality is the foundation for feeling good about life. Life feels good. Life is meaningful. Do not wait until you are old or dying to experience your spirituality. Spiritual awareness and security is for everyone. Activate your spirituality and recognize how it benefits you on your life path. You aren't here on earth to travel the journey alone, nor does the journey have to consist of fear and despair.

Embark on the easier journey. Take the high road and allow your spirituality to support and empower you on life's journey. Life is full of love and joy if only your heart and spirit are open. Open to the good in life! Move into a spiritual and emotional space of life satisfaction. It is okay to say "I love life." People may look at you funny, but you will feel good and the feeling could be contagious!

Spirituality is a necessary part of abundance.

Be open to discovering a relationship with the Universe, regardless of your age or experience. To become comfortable with something that is unknown or unfamiliar takes practice. Allow your spirituality to emerge as you move forward on your path. As it develops and matures, be attentive to your spiritual relationship. Give lovingly of your time, your talent, and your money to those who, and that which, supports your spirituality. Build a spiritual life and a spiritual community. Churches and synagogues need cash to keep their doors open for you. They have bills, too. You aren't likely to want to visit God in a cold and dark place. Communities need places to worship together. Give lovingly and generously to support your spiritual life.

Open your life to the power of the Universe. Amazing things will happen. The Universe is the ultimate giver; it gives generously and abundantly. In fact, it never stops giving. You're more likely to stop receiving before the Universe stops giving. You can turn your back on the Universe, but it will never turn its back on you.

Although you may feel angry and blame God for the hardships and struggles of life, God is still there. Clear the air with God if necessary. Despite what many people believe, it is all right—and sometimes necessary—to voice your anger and frustration to God. Write a letter to your spiritual connection, expressing your feelings. You deserve God's intended good. Open your arms and receive.

Giving is an active way of participating in life. Give your money. Give your time. Give your suggestions. Give your expertise. Just give! Give something. Give generously and unconditionally. As you give, the doors of abundance open wide to allow the good to pour into your life. Life has much to offer. Give and receive with love and gratitude for all that you have and all that is yet to be.

CHAPTER TEN

Integrity and Abundance

Always do right. This will gratify some people,
and astonish the rest.

Mark Twain

F ew people like to be told what to do or how to behave. Yet most newspapers carry syndicated advice columns that offer guidance to those who are navigating through various situations and circumstances. Most of these columns address issues related to integrity.

What is the right thing to do?

People search for the right answers to life's myriad questions, hoping to avoid making grave mistakes. We want to do the right thing. Yet we feel uncertain about the proper way to handle situations and circumstances. We look for helpful advice that will guide us in the right direction.

Integrity means doing the right thing. A person of integrity possesses a high moral standard for living. Integrity goes beyond *believing* that you are a good person to actually *being* that good person. Integrity is true to form. What you see is what you get. When given the opportunity, most of us would define ourselves as people of good integrity and moral character. But what does that really mean? You may perceive yourself as good, based on some unknown criteria. Perhaps you view yourself as kind, considerate, and hardworking. Do these qualities make you a person of good integrity?

The mere word "integrity" may be enough to remind you to be a good person. The word grabs your attention.

Although the term is used regularly, it is rarely defined. You are expected to know what integrity means. But the word leaves room for interpretation. You can't help but wonder if you truly are a person of good integrity.

Interestingly, the word "integrity" seems to be used most often around serious violations of integrity. Integrity is a value thought to be assessed and evaluated at the end of one's life. Many people therefore think that it is something to worry about later in life: *Was I a good person?*

But integrity exists in our lives on a daily basis. The decision to do right or wrong confronts you every day. "Everyday integrity" measures your ability to make good decisions for yourself and in your life. Good decisions are decisions that you are unlikely to regret later.

Demonstrate good integrity in your everyday life.

Integrity is your shadow as you walk on the path to abundance. Your shadow may lie in front of you, behind you, or on either side of you. Although it may be larger than your physical self, it is not meant to intimidate you or to scare you. You must simply be aware of your integrity as you walk forward toward your dreams and desires.

Integrity directs the flow of abundance. If you cheat others, you are inviting the Universe to cheat you out of your dreams and desires. The Universe is honest and asks you to be honest as well, in all of your choices and interactions. Integrity is honesty. It requires you to be truthful.

Integrity means that anyone who peers in on you at any given time will see only good.

Integrity permits exposure. Unlike shame, which wants to be hidden, integrity lives in the open. With integrity, there's no need to be secretive or to hide things from others. Integrity lives in the light of day. In this way, it is easy to recognize that which jeopardizes our integrity. Good integrity requires work. It doesn't simply happen. You *make* it happen.

Integrity is honesty regardless of the circumstances. It includes being honest even when you fear the negative consequences. It means that you may hurt someone's feelings and get yelled at for doing or not doing something correctly. It means that you pay for broken merchandise, and that you choose to tell the truth even when it feels uncomfortable or the situation is unpleasant.

There are as many opportunities to step out of your integrity as there are to step into it. Subtle violations of integrity are easily overlooked by most people: violations such as paying bills late or parking, in order to save time, in a space meant for disabled people.

Integrity is often exchanged for convenience. You cut through the parking lot in order to avoid a long red light at the intersection. When you're short on change, you decide not to put money in the parking meter and hope that you don't get caught. Any time that you're concerned about "getting caught," you're violating integrity. Integrity means always doing what is right, even when it is not necessarily convenient. In fact, your integrity will at times cost you convenience. You may have to go out of your way to take the shopping cart back to the store or to the cart corral. Your integrity may sometimes cause you to backtrack.

Integrity is frequently challenged during those times when you think that no one is looking. You may tell yourself that no one will notice that you accidentally dropped the napkin on the ground or threw a paper bag from your car: *It's only a paper bag. It won't matter.*

It's easy to justify a lack of integrity, to think that no one will know the difference. So you can choose to conveniently place the unwanted grocery item on the nearest shelf rather than walking it all the way back to its proper shelf. No one will know that *you* were the person who did that. You know that it's not the right thing to do. But you choose to do it anyway because it's more convenient.

A lack of integrity is also justified by the belief that "everyone does it." This belief gives people the mistaken permission to step out of their integrity. It gives people the idea that because other people do something, they too have the right to do it, even when the action is wrong. "But other people do it," they tell themselves.

That is a familiar justification that continues in many parent-child dialogues. You may have learned to plead your case based on what other people were doing. Most parents want to provide their children with a strong value system that includes integrity. They want their children to know the difference between right and wrong. Now you get to adhere to those early principles as you independently steer your life in the *right* direction.

Integrity makes good choices.

Integrity includes taking responsibility for your words and your actions. As a child, you may have blamed a sibling or friend for something that you did. You were afraid to get into trouble and so you did what came naturally: you blamed someone else. Do you continue to blame others for things that happened to you? Do you blame your professor for a bad grade? Do you blame the police officer for giving you a speeding ticket? Avoid blaming others for your decisions. You are responsible for what happens in your life, both the good and the bad. Take responsibility for your choices.

Society tends to blame the victim. However, victims also blame others for their victimization. You can't successfully move beyond victimhood if you're continually blaming others for your circumstances. Blaming others maintains your identity as a victim.

Be responsible for yourself and for your life. Learn to make good choices from the beginning. Avoid situations and experiences that surrender your integrity. If you get angry and hostile easily, take responsibility for your wounded emotions. Don't push your past and present wounds onto friends and family. They may try, but they can't fix your feelings. Take care of your emotions. If necessary, seek professional assistance in order to gain control over negative emotions before they sabotage your life course. Counseling is beneficial, but seeking it may require you to move beyond the fear and shame that typically inhibit people from receiving such a valuable service.

Accountability is a crucial part of integrity. Be accountable for your decisions and for your actions. Don't blame others for that which you choose to do or not to do. As a right of passage, you earn the ability to make your own choices. Make choices that you can live with easily and that you are willing to take full responsibility for. Police officers don't "make you" drive faster than the speed limit or pass a car in a designated no-passing lane. Despite what you might want to believe, *you* made that choice. You make choices consciously as well as unconsciously.

Unconscious decisions are more difficult to understand and even more challenging to change. When making decisions, it's helpful to ask yourself, "What is the right thing to do?" This question brings the decision into conscious awareness and guides you toward making a good decision. Make decisions based on what you know is right and not on what you think you can get away with.

Accountability is often misconstrued as blame. No one likes to be blamed; it is easier to blame others than it is to be blamed. Blaming serves as a form of self-protection. We blame others before they can blame us. Accountability is the ability to assume responsibility without the need to blame someone else.

Don't surrender to anything that is potentially harmful to you or to others, including the misuse of alcohol and drugs. If you currently use alcohol or drugs on a consistent basis, you are surrendering the responsibility for your life to a substance. Most people use recreational drugs such as marijuana or alcohol in order to disassociate themselves from negative emotions while hoping to instill a "feel good" experience.

Any excessive or prolonged use of alcohol or drugs violates your integrity. Mind-altering substances affect your ability to interact authentically with yourself and with the world. Using such substances on a prolonged basis implies that you can't manage your life alone. Drug or alcohol misuse provides a false sense of control. Substance abusers feel afraid, ashamed, and inadequate. As you move forward on the path to abundance, you will shed these negative feelings. Embrace the good in life without the use of these harmful substances.

Behave in ways that make you proud.

Integrity includes self-reliance. Many young people rely on their parents longer than good integrity suggests that they should. Integrity means having the ability to take care of oneself rather than relying on others. Self-reliance builds independence. A young bird sitting idly on a windowsill admires the sky and wonders when he'll be able to fly successfully on his own. The bird's mother continues to supply him with food for as long as he sits on the windowsill.

Younger generations have come to rely more on their parents than did previous generations. The current generation of young adults has difficulty maintaining independence. Some of them move out of their parents' home only to return to living "back home" after a short period of time. Young people, like young birds, must be courageous enough to move toward their independent lives. The umbilical cord that connects the baby to its mother is cut at birth. Life is a time of growth and preparation, followed by a period of independence.

What are you waiting for?

Too often people wait for the courage to be independent when what is truly required is risk. Risk is necessary whether or not courage is present. Fear delays the process, while risk encourages us to take a leap of faith. Take the risks necessary to be independent. Realize your potential as you move out into the world. As is true of the toddler who glances back at a reassuring parent, you must move forward knowing that emotional support is enough. There is no better way to learn something than by actually doing it. Don't wait for courage to arrive. Instead, make a move and feel courageous as you're moving. Become independent and rely on yourself.

Integrity means doing what is right, even if it causes you discomfort. Integrity means paying for an item you accidentally broke in a store even if you'd rather not pay for something you didn't intend to buy. Integrity is responding to other people's requests, such as RSVPs on invitations. Be considerate of others and tell them whether or not you'll be coming to their parties. Integrity means being true to your words. If you said you would do it, integrity dictates that you actually do it. Keep your promises. Pay people back, regardless of whether you borrowed the money from a bank or from your parents. Always pay back any money that you borrowed. Your integrity is on the line. Your word is a measure of your integrity.

Avoid borrowing money. Most bankruptcies and perpetual debt habits result from the misuse of credit cards. Credit cards provide a false sense of security. People keep credit cards "just in case." Credit cards enable you to spend beyond your means while rapidly accruing debt. Previous generations didn't have credit cards. They needed to have cash in order to purchase something your financial success depends on your ability to manage money effectively. If you spend beyond your means, you won't have any money to manage and you will rob yourself of financial success.

Spend less than you earn and save and invest your money regularly. Money can multiply in your favor (dividends) or against you (finance charges), depending on where you choose to put your money. Unless you own a credit card company, credit cards will lead you to greater financial losses than gains. Avoid falling prey to credit card debt. Use credit wisely. Credit is useful when you are purchasing a home or a business, but not when you are buying another pair of jeans on sale at the local department store.

Know the difference between a need and a want. A need is something that you require in order to live your life, such as heat in your house or a car to drive to work. A want is something that you'd like to have, but that isn't necessary for your day-to-day life. Confusion about the differences between needs and wants leads to financial difficulties.

Avoid spending money haphazardly. In other words, avoid spending money that you don't have in your physical possession. If you have not yet paid your telephone bill, don't spend money dining out on the weekends. It is a violation of integrity to spend money that actually belongs to someone else: in this example, the telephone company. Pay your bills first and enjoy peace of mind when you dine on your own dollar.

Good integrity fosters greater abundance.

Become comfortable handling money and having money in your possession. Don't be intimidated by money, lest you give it away unknowingly. You may try to get rid of it as fast as you earn it. You may even get rid of it before you earn it. The Abundance Genogram below will help you to understand your inherited beliefs and patterns regarding money. Fear and discomfort put you at risk for excessive spending. Make friends with money; allow it to be a comfortable part of your life. Money in your possession invites more money into your life. It is the key to financial success. Money is good, and it is good to have it in your possession.

Abundance is dependent upon good integrity. Be willing to walk in the light of day. In this way, when you glance over at your shadow of integrity, you can't help but smile. It feels good to do what is right and to be a person of true integrity. Integrity enhances your life and produces great returns on the path to abundance.

The Abundance Genogram.

What do you wish you had more of in your life?

The Abundance Genogram serves as a map of family relations and individual perceptions of abundance.

If you desire more money, create a Genogram for money. Review significant family members and how they viewed and used money in their lives. You can also generate a Genogram for time, relationships, and work to identify inherited patterns in your life. What was the family motto that resulted? The following is an example of a money-related Genogram:

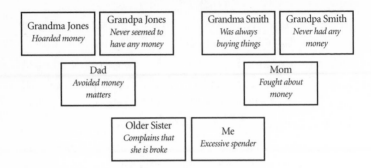

| Grandma Jones
Hoarded money | Grandpa Jones
*Never seemed to
have any money* | Grandma Smith
*Was always
buying things* | Grandpa Smith
*Never had any
money* |

| Dad
*Avoided money
matters* | Mom
*Fought about
money* |

| Older Sister
*Complains that
she is broke* | Me
Excessive spender |

Family Motto: Earn and Burn

Upon completing the Genogram, you will gain valuable insight into your own patterns. Perhaps you have unconsciously adhered to your family motto. If so, choose to create a healthier motto for your life. For instance, if the family motto was "Earn and Burn," change your motto to "Honor and Keep." In doing so, you are changing a belief that sabotages your abundance to a belief that invites abundance.

Create a Genogram for money, time, relationships, or other factors related to your abundance. Review how grandparents, parents, and siblings viewed this specific issue. Create additional boxes as needed and complete the family motto.

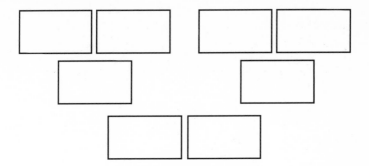

Thus your family motto is:

CHAPTER ELEVEN

Making Room for Abundance: Your Abundance Awaits Clearance

It is not how much we have, but how much we enjoy, that makes happiness.

Charles H. Spurgeon

Your abundance is now making its way to you. It began its journey in the invisible sphere and it is on the cusp of materializing into physical form. Just as expectant parents prepare a place for their anticipated new arrival, you must prepare a place for the arrival of your new bundle of joy. Abundance needs adequate space to land in your life. But where will you put it? After all, you most likely already have a lot of stuff. If you are like a lot of people, your rooms are filled with furniture, your closets are filled with clothing, and your mailbox is filled with junk mail.

It is rare to have open space in our homes and in our lives. Many people seem to believe that the purpose of open space is to fill it quickly, thereby avoiding uncomfortable feelings of fear and discontent. Open spaces give the impression that something is incomplete or unfinished; it feels as if something is lacking. Things left in an indeterminate state seem awkward and uncomfortable—feelings that prompt us to complete the project and to fill up the space. People may fill such spaces with items that are "good enough for now," until they get something better. Lots of people know how to quickly fill up empty spaces.

It can feel natural to surround yourself with material items, also referred to as "stuff." First-year college students, for example, have a tendency to pack their entire bedrooms when moving to a dormitory for the first time. Regardless of where you are in life, you may be inclined to pack and carry more than you need. You may carry a purse, a cell phone, and a checkbook into the supermarket and then go on to fill your arms and shopping baskets with more stuff.

People unnecessarily burden themselves with things. They store belongings. They buy new, but keep the old. Many people become "stuffaholics," addicted to accumulating more possessions. Material items act as a cushion that surrounds such folks with a false sense of security. They believe they feel better surrounded by stuff. But they've accumulated more than they need and more than they can possibly use. You can easily clutter your life with stuff. And, sadly, you will then have stuff instead of abundance.

Abundance needs a place to land.

Airplanes require space in order to land, something that is also true for your abundance. Abundance needs a clear and unoccupied space to land in your life. An open space communicates *availability*. It demonstrates that you are available to receive. An open space communicates *readiness*, that you are ready to receive abundance.

Abundance is energy—a moving and vibrating force that multiplies, quickly producing more energy. The energy of abundance needs space to move about freely. Abundance is expression. What goes in must come out. Intentions and words create an energy that must be expressed, and such energy is expressed positively as abundance. The expression of energy ceases to have energy when it is contained or blocked in any way. Your abundance is waiting on the perimeters of the invisible for its clearance to land.

Create the necessary space for your abundance. Clean out your home, your office, and your car. Reduce clutter. Discard those items that you no longer like, no longer use, and no longer need. Make room for abundance. Create an open space for what you want in your life. If you want a new computer, donate your old computer. If you want a new car, put a "For Sale" sign on your current car. Holding on to possessions that you no longer need creates clutter. Clutter stifles the energy of abundance.

Learn to let go in order to receive what you truly desire. Even the Space Shuttle drops what it no longer needs as it launches into space. Abundance is easily demonstrated in nature. The maple tree drops its leaves every autumn. You, too, must learn to drop the excess that you no longer need. It burdens you unnecessarily.

Discard items that are broken and in disrepair. Create the space for your desired good. Donate the scarf that you received as a Christmas gift several years ago and have yet to wear. Avoid hanging such gifts in your closet indefinitely. When you know that you're not going to wear something, get rid of it immediately. Let go and allow something else to manifest, something you actually like and want.

Clutter creates disorder and blocks your abundance. Yet a cluttered closet is often mistaken for abundance. Clutter, like abundance, speaks of more than enough. A closet overflowing with clothes, shoes, and other accessories communicates that you have more than enough. However, if your closet is like most people's closets, it is filled with clothes that you don't like, you don't wear, and that don't fit. Lots of people hold on to clothes indefinitely. They like their closets over-flowing, even though the contents are useless or out of style.

Don't justify keeping old clothes. Styles change. Preferences change. Don't keep clothes simply because they were once expensive, if they are clothes that you prefer not to wear. Fill your closet with clothes that you like, clothes that complement your appearance and that feel comfortable. These clothes are the first ones you reach for on a Monday morning when you don't want to iron or fuss. Fill your closet with clothes that you enjoy wearing, and remove everything else. When you have fewer clothes, you'll spend less time rummaging around in your closet looking for the ideal outfit.

Discard or donate.

Create space in your closet for what you want to wear. Discard or donate the rest. Give your clothes to someone who will love them and use them.

Closets collect stuff. You put an item in a closet to keep it out of sight, and then you quickly forget about it. After putting more and more stuff in the closet, the closet becomes cluttered. Clutter accumulates quickly in closets, until you can sort through the stuff and determine what you need and what you can discard. Space is sacred. It holds the place for your desired abundance, so avoid filling up this sacred space with meaningless clutter. If you don't need something, then you don't need to store it indefinitely. Discard and donate, and open the space for what you truly want.

Clothing isn't the only thing in your life that creates clutter. Paper takes up space and can also pile up quickly. Paper comes in various forms, including newspapers, forms, memos, and bills. The mail is comprised of various papers and envelopes, all of which are replenished on a daily basis. Paper multiplies and accumulates easily.

Papers rapidly clutter your home and office, taking over desks, countertops, and dining-room tables. Paper lies around indefinitely, awaiting your attention. If you can't look at a piece of paper now, you'll probably save it for a later time. If that's the case, you end up keeping papers that you have yet to look at. You hope to read that article on happy relationships, but time and clutter prevent you from doing so. And so it sits. Magazines and newspapers add to the paper pile-up. You might put magazine articles somewhere, hoping to look at them another day. Then these articles get buried beneath a pile of paper, which has to be sorted. Time continues to pass and the pile continues to grow. Soon it's necessary to start a new pile. The paper piles mount and multiply, creating more clutter.

Make your life simpler.

Reduce the clutter of papers. Handle paper items one time. Review paper information and decide either to discard the papers or to file them appropriately. Keep the bills that require attention in a specific location so that you can make timely payments. If possible, pay your monthly bills online to reduce the amount of paper in your life.

Discard receipts for items that you bought months ago. Many people keep receipts "just in case," but it isn't necessary to keep them indefinitely. Most paper can be discarded immediately. Reduce paper clutter by opening your mail next to a wastebasket, so you can easily discard unecessary paper. Adopt a quick and easy approach to clutter elimination. Eliminating clutter is easy.

Write down important dates immediately on a calendar and discard the numerous individual papers that are easily misplaced. Information that requires either immediate or future attendance needs to be organized. Don't invite struggle by relying solely on your memory. Write things down! Consider buying a PalmPilot, so that you will be able to keep track of various kinds of information in the palm of your hand.

Discard or file papers.

Fear is the culprit behind your inclination to keep stuff unnecessarily. You may hold onto things because you fear that you won't have what you need when you need it. So you keep the old and even the broken. Perhaps you keep things indefinitely, just in case you need them again at some unknown time in the future. Holding on to stuff demonstrates an underlying fear that your needs won't be met. Instead, you acquire and accumulate. If you are afraid to have less than you need, you end up buying and keeping more than you need. Fear opposes abundance. Abundance is the ability to receive your good through trust, not fear.

For some people, the tendency to accumulate stuff is related to a subconscious feeling of denial. These people compensate for that which they were previously denied. Someone who was once denied adequate clothes is at risk for collecting clothing. Someone once denied food is at risk for keeping their cupboards and pantries cluttered. They can't seem to get enough of something they were once denied. Consider this example:

Maria grew up as the youngest of six children in her family. Her wardrobe consisted of hand-me-downs from older siblings. As an adult, she has several closets filled with clothing for herself. She frequently purchases new clothing items for herself and as gifts for others. She loves clothes.

Some people unknowingly clutter their lives, hoping to obtain a sense of security. There is security in having possessions, and so many people accumulate large quantities of stuff. They surround themselves with possessions in the same way that a small child will surround himself with a security blanket. The presence of clutter provides a false sense of security.

When people feel lonely, frustrated, or sad, they may attempt to dull those feelings by buying things. They comfort themselves with food, clothing, and other material items that take over their homes and cars. There is stuff in their coat pockets and purses. The accumulation of stuff creates clutter. With time, they run out of places to put all this stuff. They choose houses with lots of closets. They buy storage containers and a shed in the backyard to store their stuff in.

We are a society that loves to accumulate. Lots of people believe that the more stuff they possess, the easier their lives will be. But more stuff means more work: more to move and more to clean, giving you less time for other interests.

Clutter complicates life.

Clutter clogs the natural flow of abundance. It creates an obstacle course that slows down abundance.

Mimi and Paul have been married for many years. Mimi describes Paul as a pack rat, a collector of everything. Paul attends auctions and makes purchases on eBay in hopes of selling items for a profit. The stuff he buys continues to accumulate and clutter the couple's home. They can no longer park in their garage due to all the stored stuff. Mimi feels overwhelmed with stuff and is ashamed to invite people to their home. Her life has been taken over by stuff.

Clutter fosters negative feelings. It is easy to feel anxious in the midst of lots of stuff. As clutter accumulates, it may feel as if the walls are closing in and your rooms are getting smaller. You feel anxious and overwhelmed, not knowing where to start and even if there will be a finish. When your home is cluttered, your mind is also cluttered. You feel confused or unsure about what to do or how to do it. You lack clarity and direction. You may feel out of sorts, and irritable and exhausted because things are in disarray.

Clutter guarantees that you will always have something left to do, something to dust, sort, or put away. Clutter looms like a dark cloud. It inhibits relaxation. It is difficult to relax when you know that there are things to do. Clutter calls out for attention day after day; you know you have to de-clutter but you can't always find the time.

Clutter costs time. It takes more time to look for things that lie beneath the clutter. You can't find car insurance papers. Items fall from shelves, and your closet doors should carry warning labels to prevent injury. Clutter invites things to fall down around you, producing familiar feelings of frustration. When physical things fall down, it can impact you emotionally; you may feel as if life is out of control. Yet some people convince themselves that they are more organized amidst the clutter. They say they know where things are. Yet they panic when their stuff is touched or moved.

Clutter takes little time to accumulate. Consequently, you may find yourself procrastinating until you can devote a block of time to the project. Time passes and the clutter stays for months or even years. The good news is that with the passage of time, the papers that once required your attention lose their importance. When you finally do sort through the pile, you find yourself relieved to discover items that can now be discarded. Time makes the elimination of the pile easier.

De-cluttering your life does not take as much time as you might think. Look around you. Choose something that you can put away right now. Take special note of how long it takes you. It doesn't take a long time. The belief that de-cluttering will take a long time prevents you from actually putting things away. When you believe that de-cluttering will take a long time, you keep putting off the project until later.

Begin today to get rid of clutter—and discover how little time it actually takes. But avoid starting a new de-cluttering project before you complete the original project you set out to finish. Let's say that your original intention was to put some books away. But as you approach your bookshelf, you realize that there is not enough space for the books. You begin to sort and reorganize the shelves in order to accommodate the misplaced books. Thus, the original project takes longer because of your decision to begin a second project.

As you let go of things that you no longer want or use, you will have the space available to put things away and you will avoid lengthy secondary projects. Make room for your abundance. Create open spaces and clear paths for its arrival. Pick things up off the floor. Designate specific places to put your things. Return items where they belong. Create the room in your life for what you truly desire. Throw stuff away regularly.

Free your space and free your time.

Abundance exists beyond the presence of stuff in your life. Abundance is greater than stuff, money, and material possessions. Abundance is about having fun. It is playful and joyous. It is laughter. Abundance means experiencing life fully. It consists of joy-filled moments during which you appreciate life. Abundance is a genuine love of life. It is the comfort of having, as well as of not having. Abundance means that you are simply content in the experience at hand. You embrace life fully. Everything you touch turns to gold. Abundance enhances your life in unimaginable ways.

Welcome, abundance! You are cleared for landing.

PART THREE

Abundance Is Fun!

CHAPTER TWELVE

Enjoying the Momentum of Abundance

Go confidently into the direction of your dreams!
Live the life you always imagined.

Henry David Thoreau

Abundance works like magic. Now you may not see it, but soon you will. Perhaps you are already beginning to reap results by putting into practice what you have read in the previous chapters. If so, the process has started.

As you began reading this book, you probably felt eager to get started on creating a life of abundance. Maybe you immediately applied the tools of the trade, and began to think differently and say things differently. You chose to move to higher ground and observe your desires from a spiritual perspective. If so, you have no doubt noticed the changes in how you think, how you feel, and how you conduct the various affairs of your life. You respond to daily experiences with trust. You let things happen. You have cleared a path for your abundance to make its way to you. And now you have knowledge and awareness that can no longer define you as a beginner.

Instead, you can be considered a self-motivator. You possess the tools that will allow you to jump onto the path to abundance with greater skill and confidence. You started the process by yourself. You did not look for, nor rely on, others' help. Self-motivators do not need a reason or another person to get them moving on the path to abundance. They simply jump on and start moving. They feel confident in their abilities and are willing to take greater risks. They are motivated by their own desire to have more in life.

Unfortunately, not everyone is a self-motivator. Some people are only motivated by others. They rely on other people for assistance or encouragement and are therefore delayed in the process. They must wait for other people. As a result, they are slow to start on the path. Although they want to jump on the path to abundance, something holds them back and they wait. What holds them back? Is it fear or uncertainty? Is it mistrust? Is it feeling unworthy or undeserving?

Perhaps they are afraid of making mistakes. Before they decide something, they want to know that they are making a good decision, that what they're doing is the right thing to do. And so they wait. They stand idly by observing others and waiting for their own good to arrive. They secretly wish that they could take the leap of faith and jump on an opportunity or experience without fear. But instead they choose to wait. And so they wait. They look like they are "wasting time," when in reality they are held back by their fears. Fear paralyzes people. Fear paralyzes dreams.

Stop waiting, and start moving instead. Avoid waiting for someone to push you onto the path. Do it yourself. Become acquainted with the path of abundance. Touch it and experience it in a simple way prior to moving forward and experiencing it in more substantial ways. Pick a tool of the trade that you're willing to try. Are you willing to verbalize in ways that support your dreams? Can you feel and experience trust? Are you willing to take action to move in the direction of your dreams?

Start with small and comfortable steps. At the very least, peek out of your comfort zone. Know that abundance is at your fingertips if you choose to experience and connect with it.

Even more simply, stop waiting for motivation to find you. You are likely to wait a long time. Some people never acquire the necessary motivation to lead a life of personal fulfillment. A lack of motivation is a common excuse for avoidance; most people prefer to say "I can't get started" rather than "I don't want to get started" or "I don't know how to get started." But the outcome is the same. It delays the process. Procrastination becomes your middle name. Motivation requires a first step that then generates the enthusiasm and primes the pump for abundance. That is when the process begins.

Action builds the momentum for abundance. Whether you look at it from the standpoint of "now or never" or "now is as good a time as any," it is never too early or too late to begin the process of abundance. *Now* is the time to walk down a path that manifests your dreams and desires. As is true of the stock market, abundance requires you to seize an opportunity in a timely manner. Opportunities come and go. Take the action necessary to move into the life of your dreams. You do not have to take what you get or settle for whatever is left over in life. Abundance means having the life that you truly desire. What are you waiting for? Stop waiting! You have the knowledge and power to create a great life for yourself.

Create a life that is both fulfilling and enjoyable.

Unfortunately, your life of abundance may still consist of periodic struggles. Struggle is a part of life and serves to redirect personal growth. Struggle has the potential to move us to a higher level of awareness. Everything happens for a reason. There is a reason why you were denied the job promotion. Open up to the Universe's plan. Its plan for your life is better than you've imagined. Trust in the Universe. Trust will guide you over life's hurdles with greater ease and grace. Open up to the divine plan of your life. Be patient. What's your hurry? Abundance is the journey and not the destination. Enjoy the journey.

Now is the time for moving toward your dreams and desires. By starting early, you can and will accomplish great things. Strive for consistency, not perfection. Although you may make occasional mistakes, know that mistakes are part of the learning curve. Accept responsibility for a mistake, repair it when necessary, and then move forward, having learned even more on your journey to abundance.

Avoid making things bigger and more difficult than they need to be. In other words, don't create struggle where there isn't any. Experiences in life are easily magnified by negative thoughts and feelings. Let experiences be what they are. Avoid the temptation to make them bigger and more difficult. Adopt the phrase "It is what it is." In doing so, you accept the circumstances and minimize negative feelings. Make small the struggles of life. Make big that which is meaningful in your life.

Life is not without struggle. However, your approach to life and your response to struggle will determine the imprint of your life. Let go of anything that doesn't serve a valuable purpose for you: material possessions as well as negative thoughts, feelings, and experiences. Approach all experiences in life in a positive and helpful way. Focus your attention on making good from every situation.

Avoid feeling discouraged. Discouragement is a feeling that will quickly lead you off course, sometimes permanently. Discouragement will sabotage your dreams and your forward movement.

How important are your dreams?

Don't surrender to feelings that are neither helpful nor permanent. Discouragement will rear its head if you feel that you've waited too long. You'll feel discouraged if you want your desires to manifest within *your* time frame and not that of the Universe. Now is a good time to review what you've done so far on your path to fulfillment. Did you enroll in a college course on your way to a degree? Did you look at house plans or talk to the bank about a mortgage? Give yourself credit for what you've already done. Too often, we climb a mountain only to see the next mountain still ahead of us. Life is a series of mountains, with many goals to be achieved. Recognize what you have accomplished thus far. Your desire to create a fulfilling life is exciting and fun.

Abundance is the fire that begins with a simple spark. Once started, abundance creates momentum. Things begin to happen, pick up speed, and manifest sooner than they did in the beginning. Consider the following:

Jamie lived in a house that she didn't love. She called contractors to get estimates on substantial renovations that she couldn't easily afford. She tried to make the house more like she had dreamed it would be, but she still felt frustrated and "stuck" in her house. She decided that she had nothing to lose by adopting the tools for abundance. Within a couple of months, she had found a house she loved in a town where she had always wanted to live. She put her house on the market to see what would happen. Was this her dream coming to fruition? Her house sold the first day it was put on the market. She then purchased the house of her dreams.

A spark is only the beginning of a fire that has the potential to burn powerfully for a long time. However, it is easier to keep a fire burning than it is to start a fire from the beginning again, which is also true of abundance. As abundance begins to materialize in your life, you will feel excited and determined. A fire requires constant attention and regular stoking. Don't allow the fire to smolder and extinguish. Stay attentive to your abundance. Continually make things happen. Avoid complacency. Don't forget to use your tools.

Abundance flows constantly;
it is the energy within you and around you.

You may forget to stoke the fire, and instead become distracted by the hectic pace of managing life's details. You could lose sight of the abundance that showers over you. You might lose your way and life could become gray and cloudy. You could forget to tap into the powerful source of good in your life. Instead, you may struggle, with your thoughts becoming negative once again. You might say things that you don't mean, and head back on the path toward old and familiar patterns. If that happens, you will be sabotaging your dreams and desires.

Everyone has the ability to sabotage their dreams and desires, to put their dreams on the back burner—with the idea of manifesting them some other day: *I'll call for college registration materials tomorrow*. Your dreams are important, and procrastination will drain your dreams of their importance. Other things will seem more important. Avoid abandoning your dreams, even if you think you are merely putting them off for only one more day or one more year.

Make your dreams a priority.

It's too easy to fill up your life with people, places, and experiences that you don't really desire. Your dreams deserve priority. Ask yourself, "Does this [event, experience, or decision] move me in the direction of my dreams?" Don't clutter your schedule with activities that take you away from your dreams. Always stay true to your dreams.

Your dreams originated in the invisible sphere where the concept of time does not exist. Your dreams are unaware that there is a particularly good time or a particularly bad time to manifest. Dreams arrive as directed by the Universe, with divine time, and the Universe determines the time when your dreams will manifest. Do not become discouraged while you wait. Do not give in to feelings that you will never find a better job or a loving relationship. Of course you will. Be patient and trust.

Trust differs from waiting, which is often associated with something negative. You may be accustomed to waiting for something bad to happen. Thus, waiting makes you feel nervous and scared; you don't like to wait. Waiting means that you aren't doing anything—it feels like lost or wasted time. You would rather do something, anything, to avoid having to wait. In avoiding the wait, you hope to avoid the fear.

Trust is the opposite of fear. Trust is waiting without fear. Trust means that you are doing something. You are trusting! Trusting is active, not passive. It requires you to sit back and see what happens. Trust is associated with good feelings; it produces calmness and serenity.

Abundance produces an array of positive feelings. It allows you to feel happy, content, worthy, and grateful. Gratitude keeps abundance flowing into your life.

Gratitude maintains the momentum of abundance.

Say "thank you." Appreciate the good that comes your way. Most importantly, appreciate what you have already manifested. Take proper care of the things that you already possess.

Take care of your home and the miscellaneous possessions in your home. Your interest in, and the action of, taking care of your possessions communicates gratitude. If you are grateful for what you own, you take care of your possessions. Gratitude invites greater abundance.

The theologian Meister Eckhart wrote that "if the only prayer you say is 'thank you,' it will be enough." Give thanks to the Universe for its generosity. You have much to be thankful for in your life, and the expression of gratitude is essential. When you give a gift to someone, you want to know that the gift was appreciated. Giving thanks is the right thing to do.

Appreciate all that comprises your life, including but not limited to your family, friends, vehicles, opportunities, and good health. There is much to be grateful for every day. Take note of all the good that already exists in your life. Be thankful for your hot shower earlier today. Imagine a day begun with a cold shower. Be thankful for the fuel in your car and for the food in your refrigerator. Be thankful for all that you have and for all that is yet to come. Embrace your good with gratitude.

Abundance is fun! It is fun to see, and it is fun to experience your desires as they materialize easily. Manifesting abundance feels amazing and magical, when in reality it is simple. It is simple to manifest your dreams and desires. It is simple to experience life as it was divinely intended. Your life is guided. The Universe is there and wants to provide you with a wealth of good.

Ask and you shall receive.

What the Universe doesn't tell you is that, despite knowing how to manifest your desires, you also remain able to sabotage them. Perhaps you know how to fill up your schedule so that you won't have time to paint, draw, or play music. You think and you wait for more time to do the things that you love. Time is simply an excuse. But everyone on this planet is given the same amount of time, twenty-four hours in a day and fifty-two weeks in a year. Time is fixed. The difference lies only in how you choose to spend your time.

How do you perceive time? Do you feel as if you have enough time or not enough time? Can you take time for yourself? Or do you feel unworthy of time and spend it foolishly? In other words, do you waste time? Time is a precious commodity in achieving abundance. Learn to take your time, as you move forward on the abundance path. Don't rush. Move at an easy pace. Notice things on your path as you move forward. If you rush, you will miss life's details. Be mindful of your surroundings, of what you do and of what you say. Stay conscious. Conscious living is abundant living. Establish your own pace for manifesting your dreams and for accomplishing great things. "Take your time" means to take the time you need. You are worthy of time. You are worthy of all good things. Take your time. Claim your good.

Examine any fear that prevents your dreams from materializing. What if people like your work? Then what? Will you be afraid at a different level? Are you afraid then that you will have to work more? Fear will readily block your path with any chance it is given. But fear is only a feeling. Fear represents another way of becoming aware and conscious. The knowledge and awareness of what holds you back or stands in your way creates the power to move you beyond it. Face your fears. Expose them and move on, living the life that you desire. Beyond fear, there is little else that will stand in the way of you manifesting your dreams.

Fear is rarely genuine. It is a sensation exemplified by the child who fearfully insists that there is a monster in the closet when there isn't a monster in the closet. Fear exists in our minds before it can actually manifest in a physical form. Stop scaring yourself. Don't be afraid. Be selective about what you read and what you watch on television. The media produces and exacerbates fear.

Avoid the tendency to make things bigger or harder than they actually are. That is fear at work. Don't let yourself think that you can't own a home or buy a new car. Don't convince yourself that you're not smart enough to have a college education. Stop believing that your new friend isn't romantically interested in you. Fear can hold you back before you ever give life a chance.

Give your dreams a chance.

Don't give into fear and abandon your hopes and dreams prematurely. Events in life are rarely as bad as fear makes them out to be. Fear prevents you from taking action. Take action instead of surrendering to the fear. There is no monster in the closet! Register for the class. Ask your friend to go to the movies. Start living beyond your fears. Don't allow fear to hold you back or to limit your abundance. Remember that abundance is natural. It surrounds you in nature, everywhere you look. Learn to merge with the abundance and enjoy your life. It doesn't take a rocket scientist or an advanced degree in manifestation. It just takes action.

Acknowledge what holds you back and then move forward. Creative people know how this process works, and what happens if they wait for someone to give them permission to work on their creative project.

Abundance is more than financial and emotional enjoyment. Abundance is having the time to enjoy the people and things you love. As you now realize, your thoughts and attitudes can get in the way of abundance. You may see the process as more challenging than it actually is, and therefore you don't pick up your pen to write, your guitar to play, or the catalog to select a class. You wait instead for the "right time."

Now is always the right time.

Opportunities and experiences won't come to you unless it's the right time. The self-saboteur within you will always imagine ways to defeat yourself and deflate your dreams. When this happens to you, step back onto the path of abundance and continue what you started. Move in the direction of your dreams, until they are fulfilled in the way you desire them to be. Do not allow anyone or anything to stand between you and the realization of your dreams. They are yours for the taking, but it is up to you to take them.

Give yourself permission to manifest and embrace your dreams. Know that you deserve such dreams. You deserve a life that you can embrace with love. Imagine waking up each morning knowing that you are spending the day doing what you love with people whom you love. That is abundance. Have a healthy desire for more—more fun, more joy, more love, and more wonderful life experiences. Choose people who encourage you to have more and to be more, not less. Be with people who are lighthearted and live life from the perspective of abundance, people who don't worry or fear for tomorrow. Such people live in and enjoy today. They have what they need and what they want. No more, no less.

Abundance works like magic. Before you couldn't see it, but now you can. At first, you couldn't see your desires materialize, but with time and knowledge that has started to change. Make use of the tools you have learned and keep this book, this toolbox, close at hand. A life of abundance awaits you. Go out and meet it. Enjoy the experience.

It is time to set your course to a life of abundance.

As the shift toward abundance begins to occur, you may feel overwhelmed by the arrival of your abundance. It can sometimes feel as if too much is happening all at once. The intensity with which the shift happens could throw you off course. You asked for abundance, you received it, and now you might feel that you can't handle it. Abundance feels overwhelming when you choose to perceive it as too much to handle. Yet it is merely the *feeling* of too much, as opposed to the *reality* of too much.

Avoid pushing abundance away or withdrawing from it when you think or feel as though it is all too much. Abundance is never too much. It's what you asked for! Be mindful of what you ask for when asking for abundance.

Ask only for what you want to have happen. When your good is flowing, manage the pace so that you don't feel overwhelmed. Recognize it for the abundance that it is and that you asked for. After all, you had to wait with trust for this abundance. Don't chase it away. Tell yourself that your desired good has arrived and that it feels good.

You are worthy of abundance. Open your arms wide and receive it fully. Abundance arrives at the right time and in the right amount. Your abundance will arrive. Buckle up. It is okay. Actually, it's better than okay. It's abundance!

Open up to all avenues and opportunities of abundance. Do things *now* rather than later. Now is almost always the right time. Things that are worth having—such as a home, a business, or an education—increase in value and therefore increase in cost. Prices will continue to climb while you are waiting to make up your mind. Build your dream house sooner rather than later. Get your education as soon as possible. Don't put off creating the life you desire. You will have far fewer regrets if you do something sooner instead of later. Too often, that which you put off for another time is never accomplished.

Never forget that abundance is possible. Abundance is not about luck or wealth, but about living the life that you desire. It goes beyond luck into a higher dimension of living. Abundance is spiritual. Abundance is your gift from the Universe. Open your arms and receive the abundance that is rightfully yours. Choose the path that directs you to your dreams and desires. Have the courage to receive what you want. View your life in terms of choices, not sacrifices.

Take pride in your accomplishments. Share your good fortune with others. Make things happen in your life. Seize opportunities regularly. Begin each day by opening up to the good of the day. You have the power to make it a good day. And you have the power to make it a good life.

Congratulations! You have just won a wonderful and abundant lifestyle! What will you do now? Where will you live? Who will you live with? What kind of car will you drive? So many choices are now within your reach. You can now create the life of your dreams.

What are you waiting for?
The time is now.
The resources are within you.

THE ABUNDANCE CREED

Abundance is my divine birthright.
I came into this world with the energy of abundance.
I am an integral part of it. It is an integral part of me.
The Universe is an eternal fountain of generosity.
It is not for me to question, judge, or resist.
It is simply mine to enjoy.
I freely share my good with others.
I now surrender the fear that has limited me thus far.
I am on my way.
I let go and trust the Universe.
I am open to all that is good.
My dreams and desires manifest with divine timing.
I want for nothing, as I have everything.
I am a free spirit, always moving toward my greatest good.
My life path is full of new opportunities and experiences.
I embrace them with gratitude.
I now see things from a different perspective.
I see my dreams through the eyes of the Universe.
I am supported in more ways than I know.
I glance down and see that the path on which I walk is a red carpet.
It was there all along, but my focus was elsewhere.
I looked everywhere but within.
My abundance lives within me.
Life is good.

APPENDIX A

Exploring Worthiness

Close your eyes and allow your mind to take you back to a time when you felt unworthy or undeserving. Of what were you unworthy? Write the experience down on paper.

1. How did this experience affect your worthiness?
2. What were the messages received from this experience?
3. How does this early experience affect you today? List the things that you feel unworthy of even now in your life.
4. Change the ending of this experience so that you get what you rightfully deserved. Create an ending in which you feel worthy and deserving.
5. What possible messages are communicated from this new experience?

Example

When I was a kid, Mom and Dad told me that they would pay me an allowance for making my bed and helping around the house. I tried hard to make my bed and to help out on a regular basis. If I forgot, they'd remind me and I'd do it with the understanding that

I was earning an allowance. Typically, though, they forgot to give me my allowance. When I reminded them about the allowance, they told me that they would give it to me later. But sometimes, "later" never came. Other times, I received my allowance and put it in a safe place in my room. When my parents were short on cash, they asked to borrow my allowance money. Sometimes they returned the money, but not always.

1. I feel as if I don't deserve to have money. Money must be earned.
2. Money may be borrowed, but it won't always be returned. If I have money, people will take it from me. I can work for money, but I might not receive it.
3. I often walk around without any money in my pocket. If I do have money, I spend it quickly. I now feel unworthy of compensation for my efforts. Other things that I feel unworthy of: payment, privacy, the ability to have my own money, a larger paycheck.
4. My parents promised me an allowance for various chores around the house. I fulfilled my responsibilities, and therefore they gave me money as promised. My parents paid me every Friday. Sometimes my parents had to borrow money from me, but they quickly repaid it as promised. It felt good to have money for them to borrow.
5. Possible messages received:
   - I deserve my earned money.
   - It is good to have money.
   - My money is always returned to me.
   - I share money knowing that it will be returned to me.

APPENDIX B

The Ideal Work Meditation

Record the following meditation onto a tape or CD for the optimal experience:

I will now close my eyes and take in several deep breaths. I will imagine myself awakening to my ideal job or career.

It's time to get ready for my ideal workday. As I wake up, I look at the clock and notice what time it is. I am preparing for the day. I notice what I'm doing to prepare for my ideal job. I head for my closet or dresser. I notice what kind of clothes I wear to this ideal job. Do I choose my clothes based on appearance, comfort, or both? I'm observing myself as I gather the things that I take to this job, if anything at all.

I leave my house and get in my car. What kind of vehicle do I drive? Is my car a particular make or color? As I drive to work, I'm noticing how long it takes me to get there. Is it a long drive or a short drive? Now I see myself pulling into my parking space. I notice the building or desirable workplace. What does it look like from the parking lot? I see myself as I get out of my car and head toward the entrance. Are there people I pass on my way to my designated workspace?

I see myself as I prepare to start working for the day. How do I choose to start my day? Now I'm entering my personal workspace. I notice my surroundings. What does my space look like? I notice any sounds or smells at this ideal job. I'm getting in touch with what I'll be doing for the day. How do I spend my mornings? I notice that time moves quickly when I'm working at my ideal job.

It's now lunchtime. How do I choose to spend my lunch? Do I eat in the office or go out for lunch? Do I eat lunch alone or do I include a colleague? Lunchtime allows me to feel renewed and rejuvenated for the rest of the workday.

I continue my ideal workday. I glance at a clock and realize that it's almost quitting time. I smile when I realize it's payday. There's an envelope waiting for me. I open it and find my paycheck for the past two weeks. I look admiringly at the numbers to the right of the dollar sign. I find it hard to believe how well I'm paid for doing something that I enjoy so much. I put the check safely away.

It's time to leave for the day. I pack up. I turn off the light. I leave the building. I get in my car. I feel good, having worked an ideal day at my ideal job! I look forward to the next ideal workday. My work is such a gift!

SUGGESTED READING

Ban Breathnach, Sarah. *Simple Abundance: A Daybook of Comfort and Joy*. New York: Warner Books, 1995.

Bolles, Richard Nelson, and Mark Emery Bolles. *What Color Is Your Parachute? 2005: A Practical Manual for Job Hunters and Career Changers*. Revised ed. Berkeley, CA: Ten Speed Press, 2004.

Carlson, Richard. *Don't Worry, Make Money: Spiritual and Practical Ways to Create Abundance and More Fun in Your Life*. New York: Hyperion, 1998.

Choquette, Sonia. *Your Heart's Desire: Instructions for Creating the Life You Really Want*. New York: Three Rivers Press, 1997.

Clason, George S. *The Richest Man in Babylon: The Success Secrets of the Ancients*. New York: Hawthorn, 1955.

Dominguez, Joseph, and Vicki Robin. *Your Money or Your Life: Transforming Your Relationship with Money and Achieving Financial Independence*. New York: Viking, 1992.

Dyer, Wayne W. *Manifest Your Destiny: The Nine Spiritual Principles for Getting Everything You Want.* New York: HarperCollins, 1997.

Gawain, Shakti. *Creative Visualization: Use the Power of Your Imagination to Create What You Want in Your Life.* San Rafael, CA: New World Library, 1995.

Hill, Napoleon. *Think and Grow Rich.* New York: Hawthorn, 1966.

Johnson, Spencer. *Who Moved My Cheese? An Amazing Way to Deal with Change in Your Work and in Your Life.* New York: Simon & Schuster, 1998.

Lore, Nicholas. *The Pathfinder: How to Choose or Change Your Career for a Lifetime of Satisfaction and Success.* New York: Fireside, 1998.

Mundis, Jerrold. *How to Get out of Debt, Stay out of Debt and Live Prosperously.* New York: Bantam Books, 1988.

Orman, Suze. *The Nine Steps to Financial Freedom.* New York: Crown Publishers, 1997.

Peterson, Ellen. *Choosing Joy, Creating Abundance: Practical Tools for Manifesting Your Desires.* St. Paul, MN: Llewellyn Publications, 2004.

Piper, Watty. *The Little Engine That Could.* New York: Grosset & Dunlap, 1978.

Ponder, Catherine. *The Dynamic Laws of Prosperity.* Camarillo, CA: DeVorss & Company, 1997.

———. *Open Your Mind to Prosperity.* Camarillo, CA: DeVorss & Company, 1984.

Ruiz, Don Miguel. *The Four Agreements: A Practical Guide to Personal Freedom.* San Rafael, CA: Amber-Allen Publishing, 1997.

Schechter, Harriet. *Let Go of Clutter.* New York: McGraw-Hill, 2001.

Tieger, Paul D., and Barbara Barron-Tieger. *Do What You Are: Discover the Perfect Career for You Through the Secrets of Personality Type.* 3rd ed. Boston: Little, Brown, 2001.

White, Carolyn J. *Debt No More: How to Get Totally Out of Debt Including Your Mortgage.* Springfield, VA: Clifton House Publishing, 1998.

Wilkinson, Bruce. *The Prayer of Jabez: Breaking Through to the Blessed Life.* Sisters, OR: Multnomah Publishers, 2000.